Chemical Evolution

An Examination of Current Ideas

Chemical Evolution
An Examination of Current Ideas

Dr. S. E. Aw
Head, Department of Nuclear Medicine
Singapore General Hospital
Formerly Associate Professor,
Department of Biochemistry
National University of Singapore

Master Books
A Division of CLP
San Diego, California

Chemical Evolution

Copyright © 1982 by S. E. Aw

First published in 1976 in the Republic of Singapore by the University Education Press.

Published by: Master Books
                  A Division of CLP
                  P. O. Box 15666
                  San Diego, California 92115

ISBN 0-89051-082-2
Library of Congress Catalog Card No. 82-70575

Cataloging in Publication Data

Aw, Swee Eng   -   S. E.

  Chemical evolution : an examination of current ideas.

  1. Chemistry. 2. Chemistry-History. I. Title.

540

ISBN-0-89051-082-2   82-70575

Cover by Colleen Dossey

Printed in the United States of America

Dedication

To

Eileen, who brought love, laughter, and
Ling-Hui and *Kian-Li*

Preface

Over the last few decades the chemistry of living systems has been worked out to its fine details. These details continue to surprise by their prolificity and novelty. An unending stream of publications on biochemical and biophysical aspects of the cell is testimony eloquent enough. It is quite apparent that an intriguing unity undergirds the phenomenon we call life. A unity that speaks of its essential biochemical consanguinity; echoing, it is surmised, a remote ancestry shrouded in the primeval vapours of the pristine Earth.

Man has sought to peer beyond that shroud from the vantage point of the present century. A. I. Oparin, as a young Russian biochemist, led the way in 1924. A host of scientists from various disciplines laboured for half a century to make that vision a reality—to repeat the miracle of the origin of life in the laboratory. In the last twenty years, beginning with Miller's epochal experiments in 1953, the pace has accelerated, spurred on by hopes of detecting life in other planets of our solar system. For the latter end a whole new field of exobiology was born. A recent cascade of books, large and small, record the ample results of these researches. Perhaps it is time to pause and take stock. This book is directed to a critical appraisal of the theoretical and applied aspects of the subject. I hope it will find, if not a congenial, at least a useful place beside the tomes I mentioned.

Several colleagues in my Department have read sections of the manuscript. The subject being what it is—controversial—I must assume responsibility for all that is written. I want to thank Miss Sorooparani for patiently converting my scribbles to typescript and Mr. George Ching for setting up the diagrams.

S. E. Aw
Singapore

Contents

Contents

Chapter 1

Portrait of a Primitive Earth

INTRODUCTION

Many believe the earth to be about 4.5×10^9 years old, and that its primary atmosphere was probably acquired at the time of its condensation out of a solar nebula. Our present atmosphere is deficient in helium, krypton, and xenon—a striking fact because of their cosmic abundance. This has led to the theory that the primary atmosphere must have been lost somehow and replaced by a secondary one. It has been supposed that neon, somewhat lighter than xenon, escaped from a relatively weak gravitational field. Evidence from spectroscopic studies of the stars is utilized in current theories of the universe's beginnings to postulate that the primitive earth's atmosphere had a high content of hydrogen, and that together with carbon, nitrogen, and oxygen this led to the formation of an abundance of methane, ammonia, and water. Miller and Orgel surmised that if neon could escape from an early weak gravitational field so could CH_4, NH_3, and H_2O since their molecular weights are similar to the atomic weight of neon.

To account for the large amounts of carbon, nitrogen, and oxygen that were retained these authors had to assume that these elements were held mainly in a chemically combined form. But equally this means that they must have been removed from the arena of gaseous chemical reactions.[1]

Free radicals, such as $\cdot CH$ and $\cdot CH_2$, interact at temperatures below 1000 C to produce acetylene and ethylene. Vaporised in the superheated steam these unsaturated hydrocarbons react with water and among themselves to yield a variety of substances, some of which, like amino acids, are the building blocks of living cells. Organic and inorganic compounds of various sorts in aqueous solution formed what Haldane termed a "hot dilute soup."

---

1. *The Origins of Life on the Earth.* Miller, S.L. and Orgel, L.D. Prentice-Hall, Inc. Englewood Cliffs, New Jersey. (1974) p. 11.

ENERGY SOURCES FOR ABIOTIC SYNTHESIS

The early Earth with its lightning, volcanoes, radioactivity, and cosmic rays appears to pose no difficulty in the way of potential sources of power to drive synthetic reactions.[2,3] However, recent estimates of the energy available 4×10^9 years ago from various sources place these as not greater than that found in the same sources in today's terrestrial environment.[4] Moreover the average or minimum values of energy flux are more relevant than the maxima as the latter would have occurred over periods that were short compared to the time required for chemical evolution. An ocean to facilitate mixing of reactants and mineral surfaces, which could possibly catalyse reactions between molecules absorbed thereon, have also been attractive aids to synthetic schemes.

A REDUCING ATMOSPHERE

Theories of the origin of life start with the assumption that the primitive atmosphere was a reducing one, or predominantly so. Only then could the contents of the "soup" be kept from oxidative destruction. Many experiments have been done in the laboratory in which chemists subjected mixtures of CH_4, NH_3, H_2, HCN, HCHO to high energy discharge (ultra-violet or electrical). Compounds more complex than those initially present, as a rule, were formed.[5-7] In the presence of oxygen there were only traces of formic acid and formamide.

---

2. Ponnamperuma, C. and Sweeney, M. (1971) in *Theory and Experiment in Exobiology*. Schwartz, A.W. (ed.) Wolters-Noordhoff Publishing. Groningen. Vol. 1, p. 1.
3. *Molecular Evolution and the Origin of Life*. Fox, S.W. and Dose, K. W. H. Freeman and Company. San Francisco. (1972) p. 34.
4. Hulett, H. R. (1969) J. Theoret. *Biol.* 24, 56.
5. Wald, C. (1965) in *Recent Progress in Photobiology*. Bowen, E. J. (ed.) Oxford.
6. Miller, S. L. (1959) in *The Origin of Life on the Earth* Oparin, A. I. (ed.) Pergamon Press, New York.
7. Lemmon, R. M. (1970) *Chem. Revs.* 70, 95.

The amount of oxygen in the air today is maintained by water and land plants utilising carbon oxide, water, and light energy, through the process of photosynthesis. Before the appearance of plant life free oxygen was presumably rare. Volcanic "outgassing" produced CO_2, H_2O, H_2, N_2, and CO and a little oxygen. Gaseous oxygen was soon lost by conversion into oxides of metals and non-metals and water. The other source of oxygen was through the photolysis of water. Water molecules are dissociable by light with wavelengths between 1500 - 2100 A. Urey suggested that this process was self-regulating and limited because the oxygen so formed tended to cut off the ultra-violet light. This is the "Urey effect." At equilibrium the rate of loss equals the rate of production of oxygen. From their calculations Berkner and Marshall concluded that oxygen concentration of the primitive atmosphere could not have exceeded 0.1% of the present atmospheric level.[8] Any oxygen formed was removed by the two processes mentioned previously. In course of time when photosynthetic life developed and flourished, under a protective shield of water, the mounting oxygen concentration soon overcame the Urey effect. The slow rise of oxygen level to the present state began.

The presence of layers of oxidised sediments ("red beds") had been explained away by Berkner and Marshall in terms of "local oxidising conditions" rather than a primeval oxygen-containing atmosphere. It was also supposed that such red-beds would be absent in really old strata. Davidson has pointed out that such oxidised beds have been found with ages in excess of 1.5 billion years, as witness the Roraima red-bed formation (~ 1.7 billion years).[9] Other examples quoted are the Lorrain formation in Ontario (2 billion years),[10] the older Muruwa formation

8. Berkner, L. V. and Marshall, L. C. (1966) *J. Atmos. Sci.* 23, 133.
9. Davidson, C. F. (1965) *Proc. Nat. Acad. Sci. U.S.* 53, 1194.
10. Frarey, M. J. (1962) *Geol. Surv. Canada Map,* 32. (Bruce Mines, Ontario).

of Guyana dated at around 2.5 billion years.[11] The immense haematite deposits as far back as the Fig Tree series of Swaziland have been dated at 3.4 billion years.

THE SHAKING OF FOUNDATIONS

a. Was there a primeval reducing atmosphere?

R. T. Brinkmann of the California Institute of Technology and Jet Propulsion has shown that the shielding by oxygen of water vapour from the dissociating influence of solar radiation is much less effective than the papers of Berkner and Marshall assert.[12] He claimed that they did not make the proper interpretation of oxygen absorption data and had assumed, incorrectly, that photodissection of H_2O becomes an inefficient oxygen-producing mechanism when O_2 absorbed a larger fraction of photons than H_2O. Making the corrections Brinkmann arrived at an oxygen concentration of a quarter or more of the present atmospheric level at 21%. With due deference to the geologic evidence of oxidised sediments he was unable to conclude that surface oxides could adequately absorb the amount of liberated oxygen. We have here an argument for an early oxidising atmosphere that preceded the arrival of photosynthetic organisms and which would, in fact, militate against their very evolution.

Van Valen has questioned some of the assumptions made by Brinkmann on the grounds of their plausibility.[13] One of these, according to Van Valen, was that half the hydrogen freed by photodissection should escape from the earth's atmosphere. In fact Brinkmann had dealt with the reasons for this assumption in detail and had also rallied support from measurements made by rockets which suggest high hydrogen concentrations in the upper atmosphere. These objections notwithstanding the merit of

---

11. Cannon, R. T. (1965) *Nature,* 205, 586.
12. Brinkmann, R. T. (1969) *J. Geophys. Res.* 74, 5355.
13. Van Valen, L. (1971) *Science,* 171, 439.

Brinkmann's paper is that he extrapolated his calculations over a range of values in regard to the parameters he had chosen. This allows room for one to assess whether his calculated results are sufficiently robust to cover the varied conditions said to obtain in primeval times. Making generous allowances for the formation of surface oxides the atmospheric level of oxygen would still be 250 times higher than the upper limit of Berkner and Marshall over 99% of geologic time.

The state of present knowledge is reflected in Miller and Orgel's invitation to the reader of their book to construct his own scenario for the time course of development of oxygen in the primitive atmosphere![14] Others blissfully continue to quote geochemical evidence to support an essentially anoxygenic atmosphere 2×10^9 years ago.[15]

b. Where has all the ammonia gone?

The importance of ammonia as a starting material in the synthesis of amino acids, purines, and other prebiotic molecules can hardly be overestimated. If Brinkmann's calculations which show the existence of quite appreciable quantities of oxygen were true, this would be incompatible with the co-existence of ammonia.[16] In pointing this out Ferris and Nicodem also set in motion a chain of arguments which jeopardises the central role which, it has long been assumed, ammonia played in evolutionary biochemistry.[17] The methane-ammonia atmosphere for the primitive earth had previously been challenged by

---

14. Ref. 1, p. 52.
15. deLey, J. and Kersters, K. (1975) in *Comprehensive Biochemistry.* Florkin, M. and Stotz, E. H. (eds.) Elsevier Scientific Publishing Co. Amsterdam. Vol. 29, Part B., p. 2.
16. Urey, H. C. (1952) *Proc. Nat. Acad. Sci. U.S.* 38, 351.
17. Ferris, J. P. and Nicodem, D. E. (1974) in *The Origin of Life and Evolutionary Biochemistry.* Dose, K., Fox, S. W., Deborin, G. A., and Pavlovskaya, T. E. (eds.) Plenum Press, New York & London, p. 107.

Rubey,[18] Holland[19], and Abelson[20]. Ferris and Nicodem have demonstrated that NH_3 is destroyed by UV light easily even in the presence of water vapour. "Hydrogen was the only gas which markedly decreased the decomposition of NH_3 . . . . If there were no high pressure (~ 50 torr) of H_2 on the primitive Earth, any NH_3 present in the primitive atmosphere would have been photolysed to N_2 in 10^6 years. For NH_3 to have had a significant role in chemical evolution, life must have formed during that geological short time period. Otherwise one must conclude that NH_3 had no role in chemical evolution."[21]

We have already noted that Hulett is of the opinion, based on his calculations, that the amounts in the primordial Earth of HCHO and HCN, two important synthetic intermediates, have been generally over-estimated.[4] He also calculated that NH_3 and HCHO acquired by the Earth passing through an interstellar cloud containing these substances would be extremely low.[22]

Hulett examined in detail the possible energy sources in the primitive environment and indicated that they could have furnished enough energy to maintain only very small concentrations of intermediates.[23] He concluded that the Oparin-Haldane model leading to the origin of life from simple components of a primitive atmosphere may be incorrect. It is certainly incomplete. The thermal synthesis of NH_3 from N_2 and H_2 requires special catalysts and high pressure to proceed at a significant rate. In the absence of catalysts the activation energy is 44 kCal mol^{-1}.[24] There

---

18. Rubey, W. W. (1955) *Geol. Soc. Amer. Spec. Paper.* 62, 631.
19. Holland, D. H. (1962) in *Petrologic Studies: A Volume to Honor A. F. Buddington.* (Engel, A. E. J., James, H. L., and Leonard, B. F. eds.) Geological Society of America, New York, p. 44.
20. Abelson, P. H. (1966) *Proc. Nat. Acad. Sci. U.S.* 55, 1365
21. Ref. 17, pp. 111, 114.
22. Hulett, H. R. (1971) *Science.* 174, 1038.
23. Ref. 4, p. 63.
24. Vancini, C. A. (1971) in *Synthesis of Ammonia* (Bogars, B. J. ed., trans. by Pirt, L.) Macmillan, London, p. 60.

also appears to be no geologic evidence, such as an unusually large proportion of carbon and hydrophobic organic molecules in the earliest rocks, that methane was ever present in large amounts. Most of the carbon is present in sedimentary rocks as carbonate, while most of the organic carbon appears to have been produced by photosynthetic organisms.

CLUES FROM SPACE

The geological record is sometimes contradictory on the nature of the primitive atmosphere.[25,26] The state of oxidation of an ore would have depended on whether it was in contact with oxygen for any length of time when it was deposited. Consequently, scientists have looked at meteorites and into the deeps of space for clues of the Earth's own origins. Mars and Venus have been popular candidates as the planets most likely to harbour some form of life, whether now or in the distant past. With the accelerated programme of space exploration now going on, it may be more prudent to wait for direct findings on the different planetary atmospheres. Inferences drawn from the present state of knowledge and extrapolated to terrestrial conditions that might have existed aeons ago do not appear to be warranted. As far as the moon is concerned, lunar samples from Tranquility Base provided no evidence for the presence of any biologically significant molecules indigenous to the lunar surface.[27] The colour of the Jovian clouds has suggested to some investigators that they could be the site of intense pre-biological activity.[28]

25. Rutten, M. G. (1962) *The Geological Aspects of the Origin of Life on Earth*. Elsevier Publishing Co., Amsterdam.
26. REf. 19.
27. *Science*, Vol. 167, No. 3918, 30th January 1970—an entire issue on the results of investigations on lunar materials brought back by the successful Apollo 11 mission. The results of the Apollo 14 mission were disappointingly similar. Ref. 34, p. 151.
28. Rasool, S. I. (1972).in *Exobiology*. Ponnamperuma, C. (ed.) North-Holland Publishing Co. Amsterdam. London. p. 369.

Alternative explanations are possible.[29] The results of the encounter between the spacecrafts Pioneer 10 and Pioneer 11 and Jupiter have been published.[30,31] The "red spot" on the planet's surface seems to be a more or less permanent vortex high in the planet's atmosphere. Theoretical considerations are on hand to support this.[32] The temperature of the atmosphere was measured at 400 K at a pressure of about 500 mbar. An immense amount of data has been obtained from the flybys by Mariner 9 of Mars[33] (November, 1971) and by Mariner 10 of Mercury[34] (March and September, 1974). They appear inhospitable to life-forms such as we know on Earth. Our views of Mars may have been deluded by its changing light and dark markings. Data beamed back by the Viking crafts which landed on Mars in July and September, 1976 reveal desert-like features and no indisputable evidence of life.[35]

The surface pressures on Venus are a hundred times greater than those on the Earth and the temperature is extremely hot ($\sim 700°K$). The atmosphere is mainly carbon dioxide with some water, but no detectable nitrogen. These findings were obtained by the landing of the Russian space probe Venera 7 in December, 1970.

HOW OLD IS LIFE?

Evolutionists mostly agree that the first life was heterotrophic and that it arose in an oxygen-free environment.[37,38] The earliest evidence of life has been

---

29. Lewis, J. and Prinn, R. G. (1970) *Science.* 169,472.
30. *Science,* Vol. 183, No. 4122, 25th January, 1974.
31. *Science,* Vol. 188, No. 4187, 2nd May, 1975.
32. Maxworthy, T. and Redekopp, L. G. (1976) *Nature.* 260, 509.
33. *J. Geophy. Res.* Vol. 78, No. 20, 10th July, 1973.
34. *J. Geophy. Res.* Vol. 80, No. 17, 10th June, 1975.
35. *Science,* Vol. 194, No. 4260, 1st October, 1976.
37. Keosian, J. (1964) *The Origin of Life.* Chapman & Hall Ltd., London.
38. Broda, E. (1970) in *Progress in Biophysics and Molecular Biology.* Butler, J. A. V. and Noble, D. (eds.) Pergamon Press, Vol. 21

placed at slightly before 3×10^9 years ago. Calvin prefers this date because of a particular specificity in the types of hydrocarbons found in certain ancient rocks which support the idea that this specificity might have been of biological origin.[39] This is the approach of organic geochemistry, appropriately called "molecular palaeontology." The possibility of an abiogenic origin for these molecular compounds has not been ruled out. The Fischer-Tropsch reaction, the polymerisation of ethylene under suitable conditions and the synthesis of polyisoprenoids in the petro-chemicals cracking furnace are examples of processes that yield discrete, linear or relatively specific compounds once thought to be characteristic of living things. "If we assume that the hydrocarbons from the Soudan Shale and Fig Tree Shale are indeed biological residues, then the whole complex of enzyme systems that give rise to them must have been generated in the relatively short time interval between 4700 million years and 3100 million years, giving only 1500 million years from the formation of the primeval earth to the presence of complex living organisms."[40] The conclusion that life began relatively soon after the formation of the earth is also reached by Albrecht and Ourisson at the end of their valuable survey of biogenic substances in sediments and fossils.[41]

DIGGING UP THE PAST—MICROFOSSILS

Barghoorn and Schopf have presented electron micrographs of several species of microfossils that they found in the Fig Tree Chert—a very old Precambrian sediment located in the border region between the Republic of South Africa and Swaziland. [42,43] L amino acids have also

39. Calvin, M. (1969) *Chemical Evolution.* Clarendon Press, Oxford.
40. Ref. 39, p. 97.
41. Albrecht, P. and Ourisson, G. (1971) *Angew. Chemie. Internat. Edit.* 10, 209.
42. Barghoorn, E. S. and Schopf, J. W. (1966) *Science,* 152, 758.
43. Schopf, J. W. and Barghoorn, E. S. (1967) *Science,* 158, 673.

been detected in this chert. Barghoorn has recently reviewed the microfossils preserved in the Fig Tree, Gunflint, and Bitter Springs formations,[44] and gives the age of the Fig Tree cherts as "in excess of 3.2 billion years." (Fig. 1.) The microfossils of the Fig Tree chert were bacterium-like and rod-shaped or coccoid. When these were compared with the morphology of those microfossils found in the Gunflint (1.7 billion years) and Bitter Springs (800 million years) cherts it was fairly evident that the younger fossils were more organised, or perhaps better preserved. Microstructures of comparable age have been identified from carbon-containing cherts of the Onver-wacht Series (3.2 billion years).[45] These were of relatively inconstant morphology and their biogenic nature is as yet uncertain.[46] However, and surprisingly, Brooks and Shaw have commented in relation to the Onverwacht micro-structures that, "they are frequently assumed to be simple procaryotic organisms which reproduced asexually prob-ably by simple division, but there is no real evidence for this and indeed many of them are more reminiscent of eucaryotic organisms."[47]

In his recent reviews of Precambrian microorganisms and the evolutionary events prior to the origin of vascular plants Schopf commented on the extreme antiquity of life. "Whether exhibiting bacterial or algal photosynthetic pathways, the biochemical complexity of these forms would seem to imply the occurrence of a substantial period of prior evolutionary development—perhaps several hundred million years in duration—apparently in-dicating that biological systems originated extremely early in earth history. Moreover, if these organisms were physiologically comparable to extant algae, their presence

44. Barghoorn, E. S. (1971) Sci. Am. 224, 30.
45. Engel, A. E. J., Nagy, B., Nagy, L. A., Engel, C. C., Kremp, G. O. W., and Drew, C. M. (1968) Science, 161, 1005.
46. Nagy, B. and Nagy, L. A. (1969) Nature, 223, 1226.
47. Origin and Development Systems. Brooks, I. and Shaw, G. Academic Press. London. (1973) p. 289.

would have resulted in the production of free atmospheric oxygen, significantly altering the presumed anoxic primitive environment and initiating the transition from an oxygen-deficient to a highly oxygenic atmosphere of later geologic time."[48] Schopf later wrote, "The oldest known rocks ($\sim 3.5 \times 10^9$ years) are comparable in age to the earliest known fossils (more than 3.1×10^9 years) . . . . Direct evidence of the beginnings and earliest evolution of living systems may not be detectable unless very ancient sediments, perhaps 3.5 to 4.25 billion years, are discovered."[49]

The discoveries of extremely old microfossils by paleontologists and new evidence for an earlier appearance of an oxidising atmosphere have pushed the origin of the first cell further back in the scale of geologic time. A period of 2 billion years or so, thought to be available for chemical evolution [37,39,50,51] has now retracted to less than a billion years. This poses an acute problem as to whether a type of microorganism such as that discovered in the Onverwacht chert, could have evolved within the time available. Mention of possibly accelerated rates of prebiological chemical evolution occur in some texts on the origin of life,[52,53] but this is no more than an attempt to side-step an issue of great importance. The possibility of an extraterrestrial origin for life on earth, essentially enshrined in the early doctrine of panspermia, argues that life originated elsewhere in the universe and was transported

48. Schopf, J. W. (1970) *Biol. Revs.* 45, 319.
49. Schopf, J. W. (1972) in *Exobiology*, Ponnamperuma, C. (ed.). North-Holland Publishing Co. Amsterdam, London, p. 16. Note: The value of 3.76 billion years by the Rb-Sr method has been applied to the Isua Iron Formation, West Greenland. Moorbath, S., O'Nions, R. K., Pankhurst, R. J. (1973) *Nature,* 245, 138.
50. *The Origin of Life.* Bernal, J. D. Weidenfeld & Nicholson. London. (1967).
51. *Biochemical Predestination.* Kenyon, D. H. and Steinman, G. McGraw Hill Book Co. (1969).
52. Ref. 51, p. 109.
53. Ref. 50, p. 76.

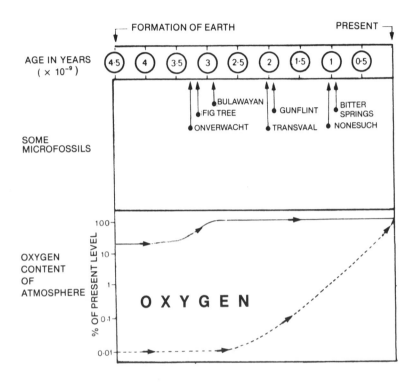

Figure 1. A time-scale of Earth's early history showing some representative fossils with their dates of origin. The lower part of the figure shows two views of the oxygen content of the primitive atmosphere. With one[8] life developed under the reducing conditions required for the formation and preservation of a soup rich in biological molecules. With the other[12] oxygen was already present to about a quarter of the present level fairly early. Biological molecules would have suffered oxidative destruction. When did the first cell originate? The Onverwacht microfossils presuppose considerable prior evolution of earlier cells.

to Earth in the form of spores. This ancient theory is generally recounted more for historical interest than to be taken seriously though, in fact, what appears to be a rather modified version, originating with Sir Robert Robinson, has lately received some credence.[54] Recent books on the origin of life, while not entirely espousing the panspermia hypothesis, leave the door open.[55,56] Doubtless the hypothesis is helped by the detection of organic molecules in comet tails, meteorites, and interstellar space. By the end of 1971 the list of molecules included H_2, HCN, CNC $\equiv$ CH, CH_3OH, HCOOH, CS, NH_2CO, SiO, OCS, CH_3CN, HNCO, $CH_3C \equiv CH$, CH_3CHO, H_2CS.[57,58] The severe limitation exerted on present theories with respect to the time factor makes it necessary to speculate that the chemical evolution of organic matter, the prelude to biogenesis on the Earth, may have occurred elsewhere in the solar system or outside it. The wheel will have turned full circle, but the problem of life's origin remains essentially unsolved.

54. Ref. 39, p. 97.
55. Ref. 1, p. 2.
56. Ref. 3, p. 286.
57. Ponnamperuma, C. (1972) The Origins of Life. Thames and Hudson, London, p. 155.
58. Donn, B. (1972) in Exobiology. Ponnamperuma, C. (ed.) North-Holland Publishing Co. Amsterdam. London, p. 431. See also paper by Klein, H. P. in same volume, p. 449.

Chapter 2

Making Life's Building Blocks in the Laboratory

AMINO ACIDS

Amino acids are the monomers from which polypeptides and proteins are made. The basic formula of an amino acid is $RNH_2CHCOOH$ where R is the side-chain conferring individuality to each acid. In general, amino acids are readily soluble in water. Tyrosine is only slightly soluble and cystine is rather insoluble, even in hot water. Amino acids are outstanding among organic compounds in having melting points which are above 200 C and in some instances 300 C. They generally decompose at or near their melting points. The amino acids found in proteins number about twenty. (Table 1) In all of these natural acids, except glycine, the carbon atom attached to the nitrogen and alpha to the carboxyl group is asymmetric. Accordingly they may exist in optically active dextro and laevo forms and optically inactive racemic mixtures. The configuration of the asymmetric groups also allows the division of amino acids into L and D series. Only L-amino acids appear to be "natural;" members of the D series may be found in much smaller quantities among bacteria, earthworms, insects, and antibiotics.[1] Recent studies of the fossil Fig Tree chert (minimum age 3.2×10^9 years) have shown the presence of L-amino acids. This appears to indicate that biological processes were active three billion years ago. The chert might have provided a stable environment in which racemisation reactions were greatly inhibited.[2] More recently evidence for the abiotic synthesis of amino acids and hydrocarbons have been found in the interior of the Murchison meteorite, a carbonaceous chondrite which fell near Murchison, Victoria, Australia, on September 28, 1969.[3] Using a combination

---

1. *Biochemistry of the Amino Acids.* Meister, A., Academic Press. New York and London. 1965. 2nd edition. Vol. 1, p. 113-117.
2. Kvenvolden, K. A., Peterson, E. and Pollock, G. E. (1969) *Nature,* 221, 141.
3. Kvenvolden, K., Lawless, J., Pering, K., Peterson, E., Flores, J., Ponnamperuma, C., Kaplan, I. R. and Moore, C. (1970) *Nature,* 228, 923.

of ion exchange chromatography, gas chromatography, and the mass spectrometer the presence of glycine, alanine, valine, proline, glutamic acid, 5-methyl alanine, and sarcosine were unequivocally established. The presence of almost equal amounts of D and L forms of valine, proline, alanine, and glutamic acid minimised the possibility of terrestrial contamination which had rendered previous reports of the presence of organic compounds in meteorites inconclusive.

SYNTHESIS OF AMINO ACIDS

The addition of hydrogen cyanide and ammonia to an aldehyde gives the corresponding amino nitrile, which may then be hydrolysed to an amino acid. For example, beginning with acetaldehyde

$$
\begin{array}{c}
CH_3 \\
| \\
CHO
\end{array}
+ HCN + NH_3 \longrightarrow
\begin{array}{c}
CH_3 \\
| \\
CHNH_2 \\
| \\
CN
\end{array}
+ H_2O
$$

$$
\begin{array}{c}
CH_3 \\
| \\
CHNH_2 \\
| \\
CN
\end{array}
+ 2H_2O \longrightarrow
\begin{array}{c}
CH_3 \\
| \\
CHNH_2 \\
| \\
COOH
\end{array}
+ NH_3
$$

DL alanine

The earliest reported synthesis was that of alanine made by Strecker in 1850. Many modifications have since been made for the optimal conditions to produce the crucial amino-nitrile intermediate.[4] The importance of the Strecker-type mechanism lies in its potential as a mechanism for the formation of specifically α-amino acids under simulated primitive earth conditions.

---

4. *Chemistry of Amino Acids.* Greenstein, J. P. and Wintz, M. John Wiley & Sons, Inc. New York and London. (1961) Vol. 1, p. 698-700.

AMINO ACIDS FROM GASEOUS MIXTURES

Gas mixtures of composition approximating to that postulated for the primitive atmosphere have been the target of energy sources in the laboratory for many years. Energy sources include shortwave (UV) radiation,[5] heat,[6] electric discharge by sparking,[7] and ionising radiation (γ rays or electrons).[8] The classical studies of Miller employ an apparatus such as that shown in Fig. 2 which simulated lightning discharges in a reducing atmosphere. By conducting the experiment over a week and by recycling the steam, enough of the volatile and non-volatile products accumulate to facilitate their detection.

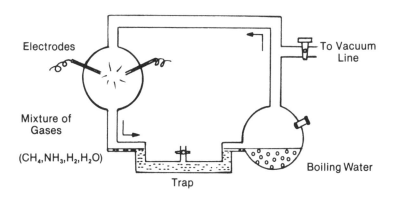

Figure 2. An apparatus which allows the circulation of volatile products through a sparking chamber. The gas mixture in the glass bulb may be varied by the addition of CO, CO_2, N_2, and H_2S.

5. Groth, W. E. and Weyssenhoff, H. V. (1957) *Angew. Chem.* 69, 681.
6. Harada, K. and Fox, S. W. (1965) in *Origins of Prebiological Systems.* Fox, S. W. (ed.) Academic Press, New York and London, p. 187.
7. Miller, S. L. (1955) *J. Am. Chem. Soc.* 77, 2351.
8. Palm, C. and Calvin, M. (1962) *J. Am. Chem. Soc.* 84, 2115.

HCN can be formed from CH_4, NH_3, and CO. Subsequent reaction between HCN and an aldehyde follows the Strecker-type mechanism. If HCHO and CH_3CHO were the main aldehydes, as indeed they often were, glycine and DL alanine would appear as the amino acids.

The intermediate aldehyde formation may not be necessary in the case of the thermal synthesis of amino acids. In the experiment of Harada and Fox when a gas mixture (CH_4, NH_3, H_2O) was passed through various solid catalysts (e.g. silica sand) in hot Vycor glass reaction tubes kept at about 1000 C, about a dozen amino acids were produced. Again glycine and alanine predominate, together comprising almost 80% of the amino acids produced. In similar experiments Lawless and Boynton also obtained β-alanine as the main products.[9]

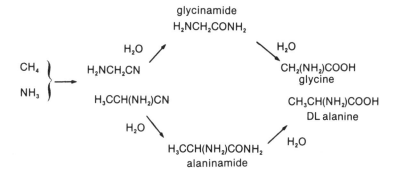

Figure 3.

9. Lawless, J. G. and Boynton, C. D. (1973) *Nature,* 243, 405.

The condensation of HCHO with glycinamide probably yields serinamide, which, in turn, can be converted to alaninamide. Hydrolysis of these amides would result in the formation of serine and alanine.

AMINO ACIDS FROM REACTIVE COMPOUNDS

Relatively simple chemical compunds can produce amino acids under suitable conditions. Valine, histidine, proline, lysine, serine, aspartic acid, glycine, asparagine were claimed to have been detected in an aqueous solution of paraformaldehyde, ferric chloride, and potassium nitrate irradiated by bright sunlight for 80 hours.[10] Several amino acids, hydroxy acids, and other biochemical compounds could be synthesised from aqueous mixtures of formaldehyde and hydroxylamine under acid as well as basic conditions by heating at 100 C or at lower temperatures.[11] The amino acids were identified by the melting points of their p-toluene-sulphonates, supplemented by gas and column chromatography. Examples of the manner in which amino acids were thermally produced from intermediates such as malic acid, hydroxyglutamic acid, glucose, and urea are discussed by Fox.[12] Under the conditions of the experiments the amino acids were polymerised and it was frequently necessary to hydrolyse the products to obtain amino acids.

A CENTRAL ROLE FOR HCN

HCN has turned out to be an extremely versatile compound in the synthesis of amino acids and other substances of biological interest (Fig. 4).

---

10. Bahadur, K. (1954) Nature, 173, 1141.
11. Oro', J., Kimball, A., Fritz, R. and Master, F. (1959) Arch. Biochem. Biophys. 85, 115.
12. Fox, S. W. (1960) Science, 132, 200.

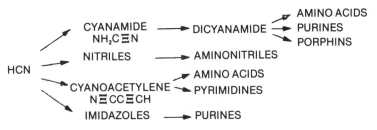

Figure 4. Production of biologically important molecules from HCN (After Lehninger).[13]

Hydrolysis of a polymer of HCN in 6N HCl yielded glycine, serine, aspartic acid, and glutamic acid. The polymerising agent was probably cyanamide or its dimer, dicyandiamide.[14] Aminomalononitrile (tetramer) was subjected to a series of experiments by Moser and his co-workers.[15,16] Alkaline or neutral hydrolysis of the polymeric products yielded as many as eleven amino acids. In the context of chemical evolution the authors were of the opinion that the reactions of diamino-malononitrile producing α-amino acids and peptides were only significant as part of the more general phenomenon of peptide synthesis from HCN and water. Aminomalononitrile would have been unstable under the basic conditions that existed in the primitive milieu. It would revert to a dimer (aminocyanocarbene) and hydrogen cyanide, which were the effective peptide formers. The prebiotic synthesis of amino acids by the attack of cyanide ion on nitriles does not appear to be feasible under the dilute conditions considered reasonable except in the cases of aspartic and glutamic acid.[17]

13. *Biochemistry.* Lehninger, A. L. Worth Publishers, Inc. New York. (1970) p. 773.
14. Sanchez, R. A., Ferris, J. P., and Orgel, L. E. (1966) *Science,* 154, 784.
15. Moser, R. E., Claggett, A. R. and Mathews, C. N. (1968) *Tetrahedron Letters,* 13, 1599.
16. Moser, R. E., Claggett, A. R. and Mathews, C. N. (1968) *ibid,* 13, 1605.
17. Wolman, Y. and Miller, S. L. (1972) *Tetrahedron Letters, 119.*

Black "azulmic acids" were formed by heating an aqueous solution of ammonium cyanide. On hydrolysis this yielded some amino acids, guanidine, glycocyamine, and 5-amino-4-imidazol-carboxamide.[18] The heating of formaldehyde, ammonia, and water under a slow flow of nitrogen at 185 C seems to have produced a similar polymer of HCN which hydrolysed to about nine amino acids with glycine predominating.[19]

CHARACTERISATION OF SYNTHETIC PRODUCTS

Most models of pre-biotic synthesis have very low yields amounting to 5% of the carbon used and usually below 1%. Methods that are both sensitive and specific are obviously necessary for identifying the ingredients of the synthetic broth.[20] The ninhydrin reaction, properly performed, is a very sensitive test for amino acids and peptides. Combined with chromatography, we have a convenient means of separating and locating the amino acid components of complex mixtures. The resolving power of chromatography varies widely from that of a run on paper in a single dimension using one solvent system to fine separations possible with a good amino acid analyser.

It is generally agreed, however, that R_f values on paper and elution times on columns are not exact means of positively identifying an amino acid. Alloisoleucine and methionine may have similar R_f values, hexamethylene- may be detected on column but not thin-layer chromatography. Contamination from handling is a hazard to contend with. A single thumb-print on a wet glass surface has yielded, on ion-exchange chromatrography, as many as twenty amino acids.[21] In addition, bacterial decarboxylation may generate its own compounds; for instance, aspartic acid forms β-alanine.

---

18. Labadie, M., Jensen, R. and Neuzil, E. (1968) Biochim. Biophys. Acta, 165, 525.
19. Oro', J., Skewes, M. B. (1965) Nature, 207, 1052.
20. Blomer, M. (1975) Angew. Chem. Internat. Edit. 14, 507.
21. Hamilton, P. B. (1965) Nature, 205, 284.

Dependable techniques have been available for working out the amino acid composition of single proteins for
over a decade. The analysis of complicated, heterogeneous mixtures is a difficult task. In examining the products
of the reaction between HCN and aqueous ammonia at
90 C for 18 hours Lowe and his colleagues resolved 75
ninhydrin positive compounds by paper chromatography.[22] This gives some indication of the complex nature
of the hydrolytic products of polymers that are created in
abiotic synthetic experiments. A startling discovery was
reported by Ferris and his colleagues in their experiments
with HCN. They hydrolysed oligomers of HCN and ran
the hydrolysates through an amino acid analyser. Peaks of
ninhydrin-positive substances were obtained. These peaks
corresponded, by their elution pattern, to the amino acids
aspartic, threonine, serine, glutamic, citrulline, glycine
(mainly), alanine, valine, isoleucine, lysine, and histidine.
Apart from citrulline, "the provisional identification of the
other amino acids was not established unequivocally by
other chemical tests." In fact, the authors further pointed
out, "preliminary gas chromatographic and mass spectral
studies indicate that, with the exception of glycine, the
major amino acids released on hydrolysis **differ con-
siderably** from those suggested by amino acid analysis."[23]
No selective synthesis of branched-chain amino acids
present in proteins occur from action of electric discharge
on a mixture of methane, nitrogen, water, and traces of
ammonia. Examination of products by gas liquid chromatography and the mass spectrometer showed that a peak
at isoleucine position on the amino acid analyser was in
fact α-hydroxy-γ-aminobutyric acid.[28] Hamilton had
already cautioned against the potential fallacy of assuming
that single peaks contain only one component and further

---

22. Lowe, C. U., Rees, M. W. and Markham, R. (1963) *Nature,* 199,
    219.
23. Ferris, J. P., Donner, D. B. and Lobo, A. P. (1973) *J. Mol. Biol.* 74,
    499.

emphasised "the hazards of identifying constituents by peak position or by overlap with known amino acids."[24] Greenstein and Winitz proposed several criteria for identifying and characterising an amino acid.[25] It may not always be possible to abide by most, or even some, of these criteria in view of the scantiness of materials available for analysis.

Lemmon compiled a list of amino acids produced in simulated "primitive-earth atmosphere" experiments during the years 1953 to 1968.[26] Of the nineteen amino acids (common and uncommon) which satisfied his criteria, glycine, alanine, β-alanine, cysteic acid, N-methylglycine, α-aminobutyric acid, N-methylalanine, aspartic acid, and glutamic acid were securely identified while the remainder were identified usually on R_f values or elution volumes from ion-exchange columns. "Amino acid products" were omitted which were merely based on ninhydrin-positive tests or approximate chromatographic positions. Table 1 lists the common amino acids which have been identified in experiments on gaseous mixtures and reactive substances.

DL Methionine was detected in a synthetic set-up in which H_2S or CH_3SH was added to methane, nitrogen, water, traces of ammonia subjected to electric discharge. Acrolein was thought to be a key intermediate.[27] Proline, valine, leucine, and isoleucine were among the amino acids formed by the action of electric discharge on a mixture of methane, nitrogen, and water with traces of ammonia. The acids were identified by ion-exchange chro-

24. Hamilton, P. B. (1968) in *Hanbook of Biochemistry,* Sober, H. A. (ed.) The Chemical Rubber Company. Section B-43.
25. Ref. 4, p. 37.
26. Lemmon, R. M. (1970) *Chem. Rev.* 70, 101.
27. Van Trump, J. E., Miller, S. L. (1972) *Science,* 178, 859.
28. Ring, D., Wolman, Y. Friedmann, N. and Miller, S. L. (1972) *Proc. Nat. Acad. Sci. U.S.A.* 69, 765.

matography and gas chromatography-mass spec-
trometry.[29]

THE SIGNIFICANCE OF ABIOTIC
SYNTHETIC EXPERIMENTS

"The very fact that primarily the biomonomers (i.e.
biologically significant compounds) rather than nearly all
conceivable kinds of other organic compounds, are
formed in the simulation procedures shows that these experiments, at least in that sense, may have pertinence to
the origin of life." So stress Kenyon and Steinman in their
text on biochemical predestination.[29] But it is fairly evident that in nearly all the work reported there has been
formed, besides amino acids, a host of other organic
substances. Kenyon and Steinman observed that, in the
sparking experiments of Miller, "other substances were
formed as well, many of which were not identified."[30]
Oro' and his colleagues similarly noted that their work
with HCHO and hydroxylamine at 100 C produced other
biochemical compounds besides amino and hydroxy
acids.[31] Sparking of methane and nitrogen gave acetylene,
diacetylene, cyanoacetylene, benzene, hydrogen cyanide
and various hydrocarbons.[14] Thus Pattee was led to conclude that "probably only a few per cent of the organic
material produced in these experiments has been identified, and there is no reason to believe that the unidentified material is biologically uninteresting or insignificant.
Perhaps the most surprising general result of all these
abiogenic syntheses is that so many complex organic and
biochemical species are produced from such simple starting materials in such a short time."[32] Cairns-Smith appropriately described the products of interaction among

---

29. *Biochemical Predestination.* Kenyon, H. D. and Steinman, G.
    McGraw Hill Book Company. (1969) p. 260, see also pp. 35, 261.
30. *ibid.* p. 32.
31. Ref. 11, p. 128.
32. Pattee, H. H. (1967) *Adv. in Enzymol.* 27, 389.

TABLE 1[a]

Class	Amino Acid	M.W.	Origin from Gaseous Mixtures	Origin from Reactive Substances
Aliphatic				
Monoaminomono-	Glycine	75	+	+
carboxylic	DL Alanine	89	+	+
	DL Valine	117	+	+
	DL Leucine	131	−	−
	DL Isoleucine	131	+	+
	DL Serine	105	+	+
	DL Threonine	119	+	+
Diaminomono-				
carboxylic	DL Lysine	146	+	+
	DL Arginine	174	−	+ [b]
Monoaminodi-				
carboxylic	DL Aspartic	133	+	+
	DL Asparagine	132	+	+
	DL Glutamic	147	+	+
	DL Glutamine	146	−	−
Sulphur-	DL Cysteine	121	Cysteic	
containing	DL Cystine	240	Acid +	+
	DL Methionine		+	−
Aromatic	DL Phenylalanine	165	+	+
	DL Tyrosine	181	+	+
Heterocyclic	DL Proline	115	+	−
	DL Hydroxy-proline	131	−	−
	DL Tryptophan	204	−	−
	DL Histidine	155	−	−

+ : detected

− : not detected

a: based on Ref. 15, 16, 26, 27, 28.

b: compound identified as arginine by circular paper chromatography.

Grossenbacher and Knight found a basic amino acid in their hydrolysate which turned out to be an uncommon amino acid (Ref. 6, p. 177). Moser, et al, reported small amounts of arginine per gram hydrolysate in their hydrolysates (Ref. 15, 16).

abiotic intermediates as "hopelessly complex 'gunks'."[33]
The primitive soup would be more accurately termed
"primitive tar." The occurrence of amino acids in the experimental "soups" is therefore not an unique event and
only in a limited sense can it be said that their presence is
pertinent to the question of the origin of life. It is noteworthy that other ninhydrin-positive compounds of
various hues have been observed in paper chromatography in areas where the twenty common amino acids are
not usually found.[34]

The physical conditions employed to influence the formation of amino acids have in some cases given rise to
controversy. An example is the discussion over the
elevated temperatures (900 - 1100 C) used by Harada and
Fox for their thermal synthesis.[35] Almost all the simulation
experiments have assumed the form of closed systems.
These place certain constraints which may tend to force
chemical reactions along certain directions; such con-
traints might not have been operative in the primitive
earth. The rapid recycling of the liquor in the reaction
vessels through sources of energy for several days would
find, one suspects, little analogy to what might have been
the real situation. Thus a hypothetical pool that provided
for the cooling of activated mixtures, so that the reactive
fragments could combine to form complex products,
would more likely lose its water through solar evaporation. Or rainfall filling the pool could dilute the constituents and lead to their loss. A site hot enough to induce
the formation of biologically important molecules could
by the same token destroy them. One can invoke the
possibility of "flash floods" carrying such molecules to the
apparent safety of the sea. The sea would be circulating its
contents by thermal convectional currents, continuously
exposing such contents to strong UV light,[36] whose

33. Cairns-Smith, A. G. (1975) *Proc. R. Soc. Lond. B.* 189, 249.
34. Ref. 6, p. 173.
35. Ref. 6, p. 194.
36. Sagan, C. (1965) Ref. 6, p. 212.

destructive propensities with regard to amino acids have not been sufficiently emphasised.[37] Amino acids absorb and are destroyed by longer wavelength radiation than that required for their production. It is pertinent to note that in the synthesis of amino acids by irradiating gaseous mixtures with UV light the non-volatile products (amino acids) accumulate in the flask where steam is generated, away from the mercury arc lamp. It ought to be apparent that the variety of amino acids claimed to have been synthesised under primitive Earth conditions comes from an accumulation of data from experiments employing a variety of reactants and conditions, some of which are mutually exclusive. As Keosian has commented, "an experiment designed to produce nucleic acids produces little else."[38]

We have already discussed the central role of HCN in synthetic schemes. But it is not enough merely to find in laboratory broths the presence of amino acids derived from HCN. The open question is the quantitative extent of the contributing reactions under the atmospheric conditions of the earth aeons ago. There are cogent arguments why the concentration of ammonia in the atmosphere would have been too low to constitute an important source of nitrogen for HCN (p. 8). Although HCN is not subject to rapid photochemical degradation, it is hydrolysed in water. Hulett has calculated that under the conditions that might have existed, the maximum average HCN concentration would be about 10^{-6} moles/litre. Evaporation from shallow ponds would not have increased concentration greatly, since HCN would have volatilised from areas of high concentration and redissolved in areas of low concentration.[39]

37. *Molecular Photobiology.* Smith, K. C. and Hanawalt, P. C. Academic Press. New York and London. (1969) p. 85.
38. Keosian, J. (1974) in *The Origin of Life and Evolutionary Biochemistry.* Dose, K., Fox, S. W., Deborin, G. H. and Pavlovskaya, T. E. (eds.) Plenum Press. New York and London. p. 221.
39. Hulett, H. R. (1969) *J. Theoret. Biol.* 24, 56.

Miller and Orgel have pointed out, on the basis of experimental results by other workers, that concentrated HCN solutions can form at temperatures around -20 C.[40] Sanchez and his colleagues have found HCN tetramers in H_2O-HCN eutectic mixture at -10 C.[41] The presence of large amounts of salts will lower the efficiency of cyanide polymerisation. In fact, Ferris and his colleagues in a later painstaking piece of work showed that it would be more correct to term cyanide condensation in basic solutions as "oligomerisation" rather than "polymerisation." Their conclusions are worth noting: "The tetramer [of HCN] is the thermodynamically most stable oligomer formed. All of these species may undergo hydrolytic and/or oxidation reduction reactions resulting in the formation of urea, oxalic acid, and numerous other, as yet unidentified, products. None of these other products is a polymer and, furthermore, peptide units are not present in these compounds."[42]

DECOMPOSITION OF THE SOUP

Studies have been made on the decomposition rates of several amino acids in 0.01M solution in sealed tubes in the absence of oxygen.[43] Serine and threonine were less stable than phenylalanine which in turn was less stable than either alanine or pyroglutamic acid. Glutamic acid tended to cyclise, forming pyrrolidonecarboxylic acid which would make it unavailable for reactions requiring glutamic acid as such. Not only heat but complex formation with the many metallic cations so freely available will tend to remove amino acids from participating in peptide

40. Miller, S. L. and Orgel, L. E. (1974) *The Origins of Life on the Earth.* Prentice-Hall, Inc. Englewood Cliffs, New Jersey. P. 106.
41. Sanchez, R. A., Ferris, J. P. and Orgel, L.E. (1967) *J. Moelc. Biol.* 30, 223.
42. Ferris, J. P., Donner, D. B. and Lobo, A. P. (1973) *J. Mol. Biol.* 74, 511.
43. Vallentyne, J. R. (1965) Ref. 6, p. 117.

formation. Glycine forms a stable copper complex. Dicarboxylic amino acids, aspartic and glutamic, form tridentate compounds with cobalt.[44] A metal can replace the hydrogen of the sulphydryl group of cysteine. This happens so readily that it is common laboratory practice to protect, with metal chelating agents, susceptible enzymes bearing these groups.

According to Calvin the time to reduce amino acids to 1/e of the initial amount, at 300 K, is about 10^9 years; at the temperature of boiling water the time drops sharply to only 10^3 years.[45]

CONCLUSION

The sum of the matter is that of the twenty L α-amino acids that are biologically essential, models simulating prebiotic synthesis have produced their racemates in the case of fifteen or so acids with greater or lesser certainty. At least three key amino acids have not been found among the products of energised gaseous mixtures or reactive substances. Upon their formation in the milieu of the primitive earth amino acids would come under strong degradative influences, making it difficult for their accumulation to permit further chemical evolution.

CARBOHYDRATES

It has been known for many years that formaldehyde in dilute aqueous alkali condenses to give a mixture of sugars. There is renewed interest in the synthesis of such sugars as ribose and deoxyribose because they are an integral part of DNA and RNA molecules.

---

44. Greenberg, D. M. (1951) In *Amino Acids and Proteins.* D. M. Greenberg (ed.) C. C. Thomas. Springfield, Illinois. p. 423.
45. Calvin, M. (1963) *Perspect. Biol. Med.* 13, 45.

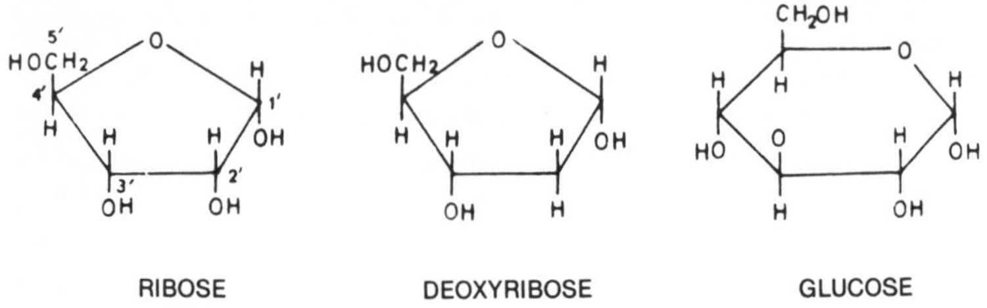

Figure 5. Structural formulae for the pentoses, ribose, and deoxyribose, and the hexose, glucose.

Carbohydrates include sugars, which form the fuel of the metabolic furnace, as well as starches, which being polymers of sugars act as energy stores, and structural materials like cellulose. Sugars have hydroxyl groups attached to a carbon backbone of variable length giving trioses (3C), tetroses (4C), pentoses (5C), and hexoses (6C). Like the amino acids the presence of asymmetric carbon atoms allows many isomeric forms to exist which are optically active. Glucose has 4 asymmetric carbons and 16 isomers are possible. Mannose and galactose are two of these which occur naturally. The D series of sugars, like the L series of amino acids, are biologically preferred.

LABORATORY SYNTHESIS

The pentoses, ribose, and deoxyribose are formed during the electron irradiation of methane, ammonia, and water.[46] Formaldehyde-^{14}C, irradiated with γ rays, formed pentoses and hexoses. A base-catalysed aldol condensation of simple aldehydes is postulated in the formation of pentoses, 2-deoxypentoses, and other mono-saccharides.[47] In one series of experiments pentoses and hexoses were found when 0.01M formaldehyde was refluxed

---

46. Ponnamperuma, C. (1965) Ref. 6, p. 221.
47. Oro', J (1965) Ref. 6, p. 137.

with alumina or kaolinite.[48] Reid and Orgel utilised the
catalytic activity of "carbonate-apatite" to form pentoses
and hexoses from 0.01M formaldehyde. They concluded
that the formose reaction as they and others have carried
it out is not a plausible model for prebiotic accumulation
of sugars. Firstly, it required concentrated solutions of formaldehyde and, secondly, the sugars formed were
decomposed quite quickly.[49]

Considerations of amino acid synthesis have over-
shadowed that of sugar synthesis. But the latter is just as
germane to a discussion on the origin of prebiological
molecules. It is surprising therefore that most texts devote
so little space to it. (Orgel has five lines on it in a book of
over 230 pages.[50]) One must attribute this to the scarcity of
experiments in this area. Also relevant are the arguments
put forward by Abelson[51] and by Hulett[39] which maintain
that much of the formaldehyde in the atmosphere or
ocean would have been destroyed. In addition it has been
pointed out that neither sugars nor their precursors would
have been stable in the presence of amino acids in the
primitive hydrosphere because amino groups readily react
with carbonyl groups on the sugars.[52]

LIPIDS

As lipids enter into the composition of the cell membranes it is lamentable that attempts at abiotic synthesis
should have neglected them in large measure. The dry
weight of a typical bacterial cell contains about 70% protein, 15% nucleic acids, 10% fatty materials (lipids and phospholipids) and about 5% of polysaccharides. Lipids may
be simple or complex and are characterised by their ready

48. Cabel, N. W. and Ponnamperuma, C. (1967) *Nature,* 216, 453.
49. Reid, C. and Orgel, L. E. (1967) *ibid,* p. 455.
50. Orgel, L. E. (1974) *The Origins of Life.* Chapman and Hall Ltd., Lon-
    don. p. 131.
51. Abelson, P. H. (1966) *Proc. Nat. Acad. Sci.* 55, 1365.
52. Fox, S. W. and Dose, K. (1972) *Molecular Evolution and the Origin
    of Life.* W. H. Freeman and Company. San Francisco. p. 106.

solubility in most organic solvents while being sparingly soluble in water. A triglyceride is a simple lipid, which, on hydrolysis, yields fatty acids and glycerol. The phospholipids, sphingolipids, and glycolipids are important complex lipids.

Some simple, monocarboxylic, saturated fatty acids are possibly of interest. As these molecules contain little oxygen and resemble hydrocarbons, their abiotic synthesis would more readily occur. The fatty acids making up the complex lipids of biological membranes contain 12 or more carbon atoms and are unsaturated at certain positions on the hydrocarbon chain. The presence of double bonds introduces cis-trans isomerism. The cis isomers, though less stable than their trans relatives, are preferred in living organisms. Presumably their configuration is essential to the proper functioning of things like membranes and chylomicrons. Palmitate, an abundant saturated fatty acid in humans, has 16 carbon atoms. The fatty acids of E. Coli consists of 12 C to 18 C saturated and 16 C or 18 C monounsaturated acids.

LABORATORY SYNTHESIS

Early experiments using the spark discharge in a simulated primitive atmosphere had produced formic, acetic, and propionic acids.[53] Oro' and his colleagues found that heating aqueous solutions of paraformaldehyde and hydroxylamine hydrochloride at moderate temperatures (80 - 100 C) resulted in the synthesis of some amino acids and formic, lactic, and glycolic acids.[54] The formation of these acids can be explained on the basis of condensation reactions involving essentially formaldehyde and amides.

Recently the synthesis was reported of 2 C and 12 C monocarboxylic acids in methane-water mixtures sub-

---

53. Miller, S. L. (1955) *J. Am. Chem. Soc.* 77, 2351.
54. Oro', J., Kimball, A., Fritz, R. and Master, F. (1959) *Arch. Biochem. Biophys.* 85, 115.

jected to a semicorona discharge for 4 days. The volatile acids, the presence of which was confirmed by their mass spectral fragmentation patterns, were acetic, propionic, butyric, isocaproic, valeric, and isovaleric acids.[55] Trace amounts of long-chain acids were also detected. The experiments failed to produce significant amounts of acids above 12 C although they yielded hydrocarbons of 16 C and above. Miller and Orgel concluded, "No satisfactory synthesis of fatty acids is at present available. The action of electric discharges on methane and water gives fairly good yields of acetic and propionic acids, but only small yields of the higher fatty acids. Furthermore, the small quantities of higher fatty acids that are found are highly branched."[56]

Since fatty acid esters of glycerol are the major components of storage fats in plants and animals it is surprising that the abiotic synthesis of glycerol has not been reported. Lemmon has suggested that this may be due to the difficulty of detecting it.[26] It is certain, however, that related compounds like glyceraldehyde and dihydroxyacetone have appeared in experiments on the synthesis of sugars. The work of Pfeil and Ruckert has demonstrated that glyceraldehyde could form from glycoaldehyde.[57]

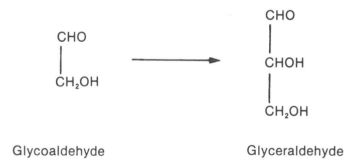

Glycoaldehyde   Glyceraldehyde

Figure 6.

55. Allen, V. W. and Ponnamperuma, C. (1967) *Curr. Mod. Biol.* 1, 24.
56. Ref. 40, p. 98.
57. Pfeil, E. and Ruckert, H. (1961) *Annalen,* 641, 121.

Another compound whose abundance in nature would make its appearance in abiotic synthetic experiments interesting is inositol. This is a cyclohexane derivative and a structural isomer of glucose. In line with ideas on the synthesis of ATP the free hydroxyl groups could be phosphorylated to yield the hexaphosphoric ester, phytic acid, whose calcium and magnesium salts have supportive functions as extracellular materials.

PURINES, PYRIMIDINES, NUCLEOSIDES, AND NUCLEOTIDES

Purines and pyrimidines, in the form of their nucleotides, are the repeating units of the nucleic acids.

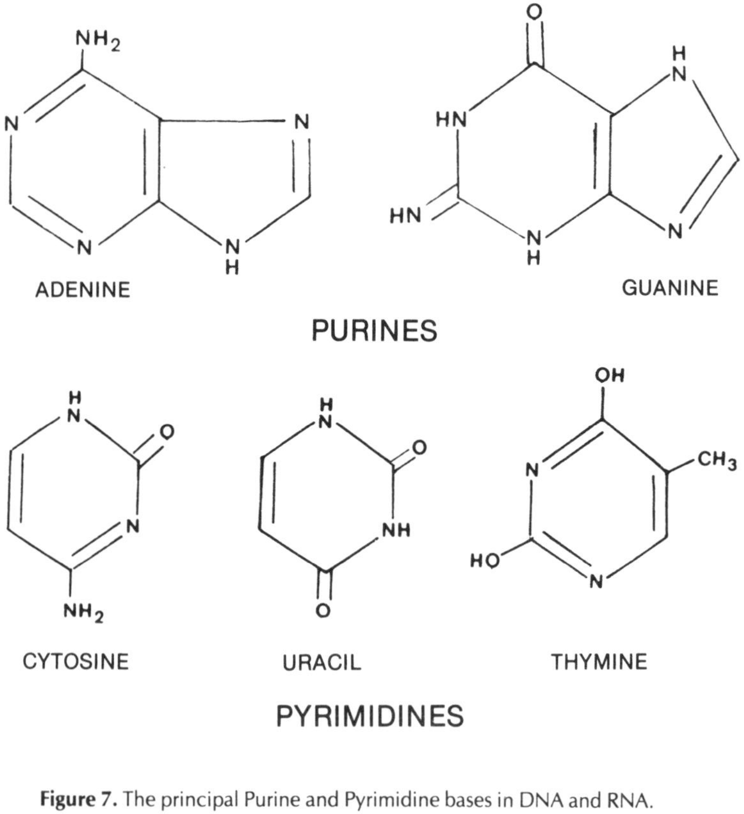

ADENINE   GUANINE

PURINES

CYTOSINE   URACIL   THYMINE

PYRIMIDINES

Figure 7. The principal Purine and Pyrimidine bases in DNA and RNA.

The nucleotides bear the same relationship to these acids (DNA, RNA) as amino acids bear to proteins. The common purines found in deoxyribonucleic acid (DNA) are adenine (A) and guanine (G) and the pyrimidines are thymine (T) and cytosine (c). Uracil (U) substitutes for thymine in ribonucleic acids (RNA); methylated and hydroxylated forms of cytosine and uracil have been reported as minor components in bacterial DNA. In RNA modified purines and pyrimidines also occur.

SYNTHESIS OF PURINES

A mixture of hydrogen cyanide (1- 15M) and aqueous ammonia allowed to stand for one or more days at moderate temperatures (25 C - 100C) produced adenine.[58] The purine was identified by eight different procedures, among which were UV spectrophotometry, melting point of its picrate, and chromatography in various solvent systems. Subsequently purine precursors, imidazole derivatives such as 4-aminoimidazole-5-carboxamide and one-carbon derivatives such as formamide and formamidine were identified.[59] Amino acids and polypeptides were also present. The mechanisms of synthesis of adenine and other purines have been worked out in detail.[59-61] Yang and Oro', using industrial nickel-iron alloy at 600°C, catalysed the synthesis of adenine, guanine, cytosine, and other nitrogenous compounds.[62]

SYNTHESIS OF PYRIMIDINES

Uracil was formed in small amounts when urea in an aqueous system condensed at 135 C with each of the

58. Oro', J. and Kimball, A. P. (1961) *Arch. Biochem. Biophys.* 94, 217.
59. Oro', J. and Kimball, A. P. (1962 *Arch. Biochem. Biophys.* 96, 293.
60. Sanchez, R., Ferris, J. and Orgel, L. E. (1966) *Science,* 153, 72.
61. Sanchez, R. A., Ferris, J. P. and Orgel, L. E. (1968) *J. Mol. Biol.* 38, 121.
62. Yang, C. C. and Oro', J. (1971) in *Chemical Evolution and the Origin of Life.* Buvet, R. and Ponnamperuma, C. (eds.) North-Holland Publishing Co., Vol. 1, p. 152.

following intermediates, acrylonitrile, β-aminopropioni-trile, and aminopropionamide. Uracil was identified by chromatography and spectrophotometry.[47] Cyanoacety-lene can be formed from a mixture of nitrogen and methane aided by an electric discharge. Cyanate can arise from the hydrolysis of cyanoacetylene, the first hydrolysis product being cyanoformamide. Cyanoacetylene and cyanate react in relatively dilute solutions at pH 8 and at room temperature to give good yields of cytosine.[63] Uracil is easily obtained in good yield by the hydrolysis of cytosine. D-Ribose and D-arabinose react with cyanamide and cyanoacetylene in aqueous solution to give α-cytidine and β-arabinosylcytosine, respectively.[64] These isomerise upon irradiation with UV light to form β-cytidine but in 5% yields. Sanchez and Orgel con-cluded, ''Pyrimidine nucleotides in contemporary ribonucleic acids are β-ribosides, and so we can only speculate if compounds such as α-cytidine and β-ara-binosylcytosine might have contributed to the prebiotic evolution of nucleic acids. The photochemical isomerisa-tion reactions, although relatively inefficient, would have provided small amounts of β-ribosides.'' There is no recorded abiotic synthesis of the pyrimidine thymine.[26]

The gross structures of some nucleosides and nucleotides are outlined in Table 2. In nucleosides the C 1 atom of the pentose is linked by a glycosidic bond to nitrogen atom N 1 of the pyrimidine, or N 9 of a purine. The molecular structure of adenosine 5-monophosphate is given in Fig. 8. Depending on the nature of the pentose there are ribonucleosides and deoxyribonucleosides Among deoxynucleotides that occur in the free form of the cell the position of the phosphoryl ester bond on the pentose is mainly on the 5th carbon atom. The 3'deoxyri-bonucleotides are also found. With 3 possible positions in

63. Ferris, J. P., Sanchez, R. A. and Orgel, L. E. (1968) *J. Mol. Biol.* 33, 693.
64. Sanchez, R. A. and Orgel, L. E. (1970) *J. Mol. Biol.* 47, 531.

TABLE 2

Nucleosides and Nucleotides

Term	Structure and Example
Base	Purine or pyrimidine, e.g. adenine, thymine.
Nucleosides	Base - Ribose (or Deoxyribose) e.g. adenosine, deoxyadenosine, guanosine.
Nucleotides	
Nucleoside 5′ Monophosphates	Base - Ribose - Phosphate e.g. Adenosine 5′ monophosphate (Fig. 8).
Nucleoside 5′ Diphosphates	Base - Ribose - Phosphate - Phosphate e.g. adenosine diphosphate, uridine diphosphate.
Nucleoside 5′ Triphosphate	Base - Ribose - Phosphate - Phosphate -Phosphate e.g. adenosine triphosphate, guanosine triphosphate.

Note: The deoxyribose analogues of nucleosides mono, di, and triphosphate are dAMP, dADP, and dATP.

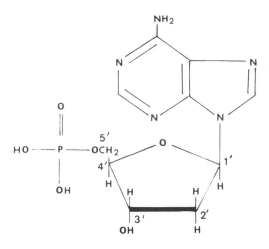

Figure 8. Adenosine 5′ Monophosphate (a deoxyribonucleotide)

ribose that can esterify with phosphoric acid, 2', 3', and 5' ribonucleotides are all found as hydrolytic products of RNA.

The nucleoside di- and triphosphates have important functions. The diphosphates, for instance, are part of important co-enzymes such as uridine diphosphate glucose and cytidine diphosphate choline. The triphosphates serve as carriers of energy in their phosphate groups, which may be utilised for biosynthetic reactions, as well as themselves being energy-rich precursors of mononucleotide units in the synthesis of RNA.

SYNTHESIS OF PURINE NUCLEOSIDES

Orgel and his colleagues carried out experiments to form adducts of purines and D-ribose. Reactions were unsuccessful in aqueous solutions over a range of concentrations, temperatures, and pH. Heating the bases and sugars in a dry mixture produced nucleosides and adenine and guanine.[64] Diribosides were also formed. When magnesium and polyphosphates were present an interesting product, though present in low yield, was 9-D-ribopyranosyladenine (presumably both α and β anomers).

SYNTHESIS OF NUCLEOTIDES

Dilute solutions of labelled adenine, adenosine, and adenosine monophosphate were sealed in aqueous solution in "Vycor" tubes with approximately stoichiometric quantities of ribose, phosphoric acid, and ethyl metaphosphate.[65] Ethyl metaphosphate has been reported to activate carbonyl, hydroxyl, and amino groups.[66] Analyses of the products of the reaction by paper chromatography, autoradiography, and UV absorption showed that with

---

65. Ponnamperuma, C., Sagan, C. and Mariner, R. (1963) *Nature,* 199, 222.
66. Schramm, G., Grotsch, H., and Pollmann, W. (1964) *Angew. Chem.* 1, 1.

adenine as the starting material, adenosine, AMP, ADP, and ATP were produced. Separations using thin-layer and ion-exchange chromatography confirmed the result obtained with paper chromatography. A later investigation reported the synthesis of deoxyadenosine with adenine, deoxyribose, $(NH_4)H_2PO_4$ and NaCN at room temperature in evacuated "Vycor" tubes.[67] UV radiation was not essential but appeared to enhance the yield. Studies on the stability of the compounds in alkaline conditions cast some doubt as to whether they were the natural nucleosides which they resemble chromatographically.[68] Furthermore the substitution of adenine by any one of the other nucleic acid bases led to no detectable nucleoside formation.[69] The polymerisation of thymidine-5-monophosphate (TMP) has been achieved in aqueous solutions using imidazole to promote the reaction. Enzymatic breakdown by snake venom phosphodiesterase resulted in the formation of TMP.[70] This indicates that the principal type of bonding in the oligomer is the biologically significant 3'-5' phosphodiester linkage. Ironically the biologically significant nucleotide is not TMP but dTTP. In any case TMP has not been identified as a product of prebiotic synthetic experiments, and dTMP is formed by a unique and complicated enzymatic pathway from dCDP. In biochemistry texts this is given as dCDP ➡ dCMP ➡ dUMP ➡ dTMP. Experiments with dAMP and dGMP by the authors did not produce similar results.

The synthesis of ATP has been shown to work only in a non-polar solvent, using ethyl metaphosphate as condensing agent (see p. 154). This reagent is prepared by dissolving phosphorous pentoxide in ethyl ether and refluxing the solution for several hours in chloroform.[66] The excess solvent is evaporated under vacuum, leaving a syrupy residue of ethyl metaphosphate.

---

67. Ponnamperuma, C. and Mack, R. (1965) *Science*, 148, 1221.
68. Beck, A., Lohrmann, R. and Orgel, L. E. (1967) *Science*, 157, 952.
69. Lohrmann, R. and Orgel, L. E. (1968) *Science*, 161, 64.
70. Ibanez, J., Kimball, A. P. and Oro', J. (1971) Ref. 62, p. 171.

Dry heating of nucleosides with inorganic phosphates, particularly with acid salts such as $NaH_2PO_4 \cdot H_2O$ and Ca $(H_2PO_4)_2$ have given nucleotides. At a temperature of 160 C after 2 hours 2', 3', 5', and cyclic 2'3'-monophosphates were found among the reaction products.[67] Uridine phosphate may be obtained by heating uridine with inorganic phosphates for nine months at 65 C.[68] More recently there have been reports of the phosphorylation of uridine with inorganic phosphate in aqueous conditions. The following condensing agents were used: cyanogen, cyanoformamide, cyanate, cyanamide, thioformate, ethylisocyanide, and a water-soluble carbodiimide. The yields were always small, even when a large excess of condensing agents was used.[69]

There has been a revival of interest in the use of polyphosphoric acids. Polyphosphates may be formed from orthophosphates by means of condensing agents such as potassium cyanate,[71] or by rapidly cooling a melt of NaH_2PO_4 held at 650 C for 4 hours.[72] Significantly the heating of the common hydroxylapatite, di- and tribasic phosphates produced no polyphosphates.[73] Refluxing adenosine with water-soluble salts of polyphosphates for 4 to 6 hours resulted in the synthesis of 2', 3', and 5' adenosine monophosphates.[72] Polyphosphates are stable in aqueous solutions at pH 7 and at 25 C. They are degraded at higher temperatures, higher hydrogen ion concentrations, and in the presence of cations. But the reagent holds good promise. Already substantial amounts of nucleoside mono-, di-, tri-, and polyphosphates have been formed and identified.[74] These reactions were carried out at low temperatures (0 - 22 C) with purine ribonu-

71. Beck, A. and Orgel, L. E. (1965) *Proc. Natl. Acad. Sci. U.S.* 54, 664.
72. Schwartz, A. and Ponnamperuma, C. (1968) *Nature*, 218, 443.
73. Rabinowitz, J., Chang, S., Ponnamperuma, C. (1968) *Nature*, 218, 442.
74. Waehneldt, T. V. and Fox, S. W. (1976) *Biochim. Biophys. Acta*, 134, 1.

cleosides and pyrimidine deoxyribonucleosides. It was noted, however, that the phosphorylation of purine deoxyribonucleosides with polyphosphoric acid, even at temperatures below 0 C, yielded dark brown or black tars.

The role of apatites in the phosphorylation of nucleotides has been studied by Neuman and his colleagues. The conversions of AMP to ADP and of ADP to ATP were brought about by pyrophosphate absorbed on the surface of apatite crystals caused by alternating wetting and drying, as might have occurred on the primordial seashores.[75,76] The outstanding problem has been noted by Steinman, "it is difficult to visualise how the 3'-5' phosphodiester linkage found in nucleic acids could have been specifically generated under prebiotic conditions."[77]

PORPHYRINS

Pyrrole is a planar heterocyclic compound with the following structure:

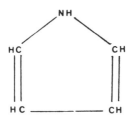

---

75. Neuman, M. W., Neuman, W. F. and Lane K. (1970) *Curr. Mod. Biol.* 3, 277.
76. Neuman, M. W., Neuman, W. F. and Burton, F. G. (1970) *Curr. Mod. Biol.* 3, 69.
77. Steinman, G. (1971) in *Prebiotic and Biochemical Evolution.* Kimball, A. P. and Oro', J. North-Holland Publishing Co. Amsterdam-London. p. 31.

Four of these molecules combine to form tetrapyrroles or porphyrins which have a very important role in biology (Fig. 9). The pigment in red blood cells which carry oxygen is a porphyrin molecule with iron in the centre of the tetrapyrrolic ring. Cytochromes, catalase, and peroxidases are all iron porphyrin-protein complexes. The photosynthetic pigment, chlorophyll, on the other hand contains magnesium. The biological activity of porphyrins depends on the kinds of side chains and the order they are arranged on the periphery of the ring, the metal chelated by the porphyrin, or the protein to which the porphyrin is attached as well as, in some cases, the incorporation of the complex into functional subcellular units such as chloroplasts or mitochondria.[78]

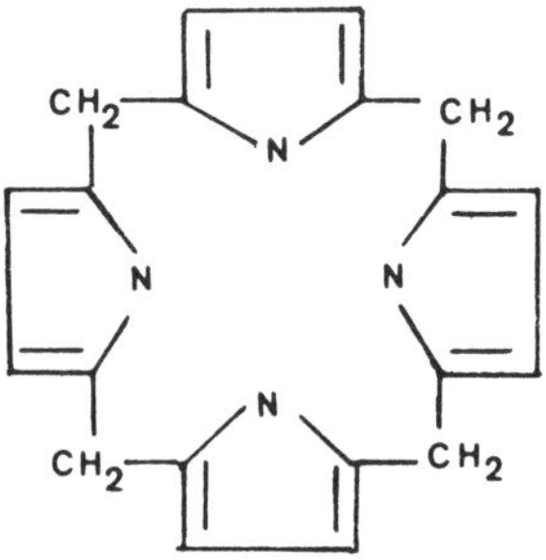

Figure 9. Porphyrinogen skeleton. A porphyrin in which the bridges between the pyrrole rings are all in the reduced state.

Animals can make porphyrins from succinyl coenzyme A and glycine. 5-aminolevulinate is the intermediate formed by these two precursors, in a condensation catalysed by 5-aminolevulinate synthetase. 2 molecules of 5-aminolevulinate condense to form porphobilinogen; 4 molecules of porphobilinogen then form uroporphyrinogen.

78. Bogorad, L. (1963) in *The Biogenesis of Natural Compounds*. P. Bernfeld (ed.) Pergamon Press. p. 183.

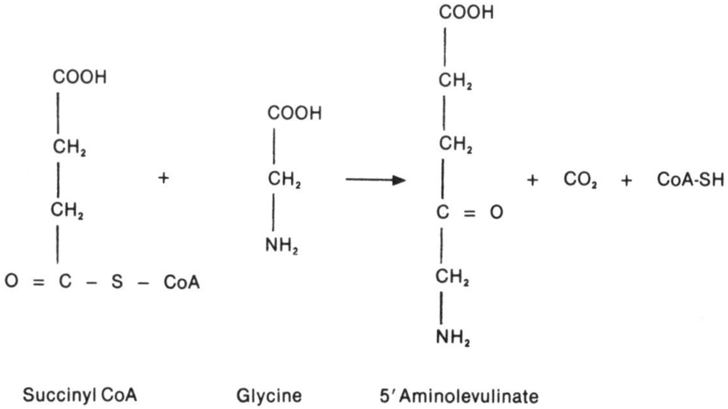

Figure 10.

LABORATORY SYNTHESIS

An attempt was made to convert 5-aminolevulinate into porphyrins by UV irradiation in an alkaline medium. Some pyrrolic compunds were produced but their identities were not definitely established.[79] 5-aminolevulinate has been sought, but not found, as a product of the irradiation of CH_4-NH_3-H_2O mixtures.[80] Experiments have also been done to show that porphyrins can be generated by the catalysis of divalent cations acting on low concentrations of pyrrole and formaldehyde.[81] Nickel and copper promoted the formation of the porphyrins while neither ferrous nor ferric ions were of any help. The porphyrins formed under simulated geochemical conditions had spectra that were different from those of the biogenic pigments, the peaks of adsorption being about 100 A lower for the latter. Microgram quantities of free-base porphyrins were generated with electric discharge in CH_4-

79. Szutka, A. (1966) *Nature,* 212, 401.
80. Ref. 26, p. 95.
81. Hodgson, G. W. and Baker, B. L. (1967) *Nature,* 216, 29.

NH_3-H_2O systems.[82] The pigments were fully characterised as porphyrins by their adsorption spectra, chromatographic behaviour, solvent partition properties, metal
complexing and fluorescence spectra. Minute amounts of
porphyrins were detected in lunar dust, but it was probably that they were synthesised from rocket fuel during the
landing of the lunar module.[83]

THE SIGNIFICANCE OF PORPHYRINS

It has been often pointed out that the appearance of
porphyrins was crucial to the progress of chemical evolution. The following reasons have been adduced.
1. When low oxygen concentrations began to appear in
    the atmosphere those anaerobic "organisms" which
    survived were the ones that were able to reduce any
    lethal molecular oxygen directly and quickly. This
    reduction was achieved by specific oxidases (possibly
    luciferase),[84] which led to the production of hydrogen
    peroxide or some organic peroxide radical. A coupled
    reaction, therefore, by a peroxidase to remove the
    peroxide was needed. It was already known that ferric
    ions, incorporated into tetrapyrroles, promoted their
    ability to decompose H_2O_2 by a factor of over a thous-
    andfold.[85] Fe^{3+} produces oxygen from H_2O_2 at a rate
    of $10^{-5}M^{-1}sec^{-1}$ at O C, haem at $10^{-2}M^{-1}sec^{-1}$, catalase
    at $10^5 - 10^7M^{-1}sec^{-1}$.[86] It was this "selective advantage"
    that tended to bring about the evolution of the iron-
    porphyrins in the capacity of peroxidases. As more
    oxygen appeared, a catalase-type of enzyme was pre-

---

82. Hodgson, G. W. and Ponnamperuma, C. (1968) *Proc. Natl. Acad.
    Sci. U.S.* 59, 22.
83. Hodgson, G. W., Peterson, E., Kvenvolden, K. A., Bunnenberg, E.,
    Halpern, B. and Ponnamperuma, C. (1970) *Science,* 167, 763.
84. McElroy, W. D. and Seliger, H. H. (1963) in *Evolutionary
    Biochemistry.* A. I. Oparin (ed.) Pergamon Press. p. 158. The opin-
    ion that bioluminescence is a biochemical "rudiment" was not
    shared by all present at the symposium. p. 167.
85. Calvin, M. (1961/62) *Perspect. Biol. Med.* 5, 399.
86. Szutka, A. (1965) Ref. 6, p. 243.

ferred over an oxidase that gave free H_2O_2 as a by-product. Here, too, the iron porphyrins are said to have acquired the ability to activate oxygen for accepting electrons directly, so that no H_2O_2 is formed.

2. The gain in atmospheric ozone, when oxygenating conditions set in, meant the loss of UV radiation of short wavelength (∼ 200 mu). The presence of iron porphyrins was necessary for the greater efficiency of harvesting light at longer wavelengths.

In proposing the hypothesis that selection pressure favoured the acquisition of an efficient peroxide remover and photocatalyst in the iron-porphyrin system several anomalies have to be explained.

1. Szutka has shown that porphine-like substances could only be synthesised in the presence of free oxygen.[86] The question then arises as to whether the amount of oxygen initially released into the environment could induce the synthesis of iron-porphyrins sufficiently so as to offset the oxygen's own deleterious effects on the primitive "organism."

2. Oparin has suggested that the porphyrins made their appearance later than adenine and flavins.[87] This appears to be borne out by the fact that the majority of modern anaerobes lack porphyrins, preferring flavin enzymes for hydrogen transport. This view should be compared with the argument developed by McElroy and Seliger presented earlier.[84] The validity of the argument based on selective advantage is further weakened by the fact that the metal ion-containing heterogenous systems so freely available possess marked peroxidase activities. Among these may be numbered amorphous ferric hydroxide, magnesium hydroxide, aluminium hydroxide, zinc hydroxide, copper hydroxide, and metal ferrocyanides.[85] Certain mixed metal hydroxides have been reported to have

87. Oparin, A. I. (1968) *Genesis and Evolutionary Development of Life.* Academic Press. p. 165.

especially high peroxidase activities. Metal ions themselves have peroxidase activity and while this is of several magnitudes lower than that of porphyrin-metal chelates, it would be reasonable to suppose that their very abundance and ubiquity in the primeval broth were sufficient to overcome their catalytic sluggishness. Were the primitive protobionts **strict anaerobes** it would not do for them to contain iron-porphyrin peroxidases since these peroxidases, in addition to the peroxidatic molecules listed above, will be lethal through the oxygen they produce.

3. The theory has been proposed that oxygen began to accumulate because of the activity of primitive photosynthesising prokaryotes, which were ancestral to photosynthetic bacteria and blue-green algae.[88,89] Not all photosynthetic cells are green of course, but oxygen producers must have chlorophyll a.[90] We are thus faced with the quandary compounded by the necessity of having to satisfy mutually exclusive postulates. Iron-containing porphyrins are said to be needed to reduce molecular oxygen to ensure the survival of the strictly anaerobic organisms then existing. Unless one makes the further assumption that photosynthetic bacteria were not derived from, or operating in, the same milieu as anaerobic organisms, one is forced to conclude that selection pressures acting on one type of organism in antiquity created porphyrins both to produce oxygen and to destroy it. To assume that photosynthetic bacteria and the anaerobic fermentors arose independently and developed side by side would seem a reasonable way out. But this opens the door to the implication that life had a polyphyletic

88. Berkner, L. V. and Marshall, L. C. (1965) *Proc. Natl. Acad. Sci. U.S.* 53, 1215.
89. Olson, J. M. (1970) *Science,* 168, 438.
90. *Basic Biological Chemistry.* Mahler, H. R. and Cordes, E. H. Harper and Row, New York, Evanston, and London. (1968) p. 298.

origin. This runs counter to the dogma, the principal conclusion from comparative biochemistry, namely, that life has a basic unity because of its origin from a single primordial entity.[91]

Plainly the origin and role of porphyrins is something of an enigma at the moment; but the issue is of importance to present thinking on chemical evolution.

91. Brodan, E. (1970) in *Progress in Biophysics and Molecular Biology.* Butler, J. A. V., and Noble, D. (eds) Pergamon Press, Vol. 21. p. 143.

Chapter 3

The Genetic Code

What makes the origin of life and of the genetic code a disturbing riddle is this: the genetic code is without any biological function unless it is translated; that is, unless it leads to the synthesis of the proteins whose structure is laid down by the code. But, as Monod points out, the machinery by which the cell [at least the nonprimitive cell which is the only one we know] translates the code "consists of at least fifty macromolecular components **which are themselves coded in DNA**" *[Monod].*[1]*Thus the code cannot be translated except by using certain products of its translation. This constitutes a really baffling circle: a vicious circle, it seems, for any attempt to form a model, or theory, of the genesis of the genetic code.*

Karl Popper (1974)[2]

POLYNUCLEOTIDES

The abiotic synthesis of purines, pyrimidines, nucleosides, and nucleotides has been dealt with in Chapter 2. In this section we will attempt to review current thinking on the origin of DNA, RNA, and the genetic code. Native DNA molecules are polynucleotides of high molecular weight (10^6 to 62×10^6). The molecular weights of RNA lie in the range of $1 \cdot 2 \times 10^6$. Soluble RNA is smaller, having a molecular weight of about 25,000 equivalent to about 80 nucleotide residues. RNA, but not DNA, is hydrolysed to mononucleotides with alkali at room temperature. These relative labilities have been ascribed to the presence and absence, respectively, of a hydroxyl group at $C'2$. The technical problems encountered in the chemical synthesis of polynucleotides have been dealt with in a recent volume.[3]

---

1. *Chance and Necessity.*Monod, J. Knopt, New York. (1971) p. 143.
2. Popper, K. R. in *Studies in the Philosophy of Biology.* Ayala, F. J. and Dobzhansky, T. (eds.) Macmillan. (1974) p. 259.
3. *Organic Chemistry of Nucleic Acids.* Kochetkov, N. K. and Budovskii, E. I. (eds.). Translated by Haigh, B. Plenum Press. London and New York (1971) Part A.

DNA has only two hydroxyl functions, those at 3'C and 5'C, to which phosphate groups may be esterified. Both DNA and RNA are built up of large numbers of nucleotides (either deoxyribonucleotides or ribonucleotides) linked to one another in linear fashion. One mononucleotide is linked to the next by a phosphodiester bridge be tween the 3'-hydroxyl group of the pentose moiety on one nucleotide and the 5'-hydroxyl group of the pentose of the next. The diagram shows how part of a DNA chain is built up, but it could also represent RNA structure since inter-nucleotide links of RNA involve 3' rather than 2'-hydroxyls. There is, therefore, an alternating sequence of pentose and phosphoric acid groups forming a backbone from which the purine and pyrimidine bases project from their attachment to the pentoses.

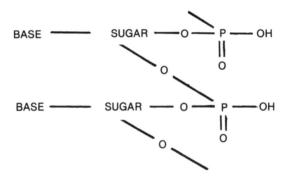

Figure 11.

The over-all structure is akin to a polypeptide with its side-chains. Like a polypeptide chain there is a "head" and a "tail" to each strand. At the head terminal of natural DNA the 5'-hydroxyl is phosphorylated because DNA is biosynthesised enzymatically from nucleoside-5'-triphosphates. At the tail end of the same strand the 3'-hydroxyl is free. It follows that the complementary strands of a double helix must go in a 3'5' sequence in one strand and in a 5'3' direction in the other (Fig. 11).

While the secondary structure of DNA is usually a double-stranded helix, the RNA as well as DNA of certain viruses occur as single polynucleotide chains. The DNA of the mature $\phi \times 174$ is in the form of a ring of nearly 4,500 deoxyribonucleotides. DNA from prokaryotes and the mitochondria of some cells are found in the form of covalently linked circles. Recently mitochondrial DNA has been seen as concatenated structures, which are short chains of linked circles of DNA resembling a daisy chain.[4] In the double helix of DNA the adenine (A) of one strand is hydrogen-bonded to thymine (T) in the other, and cytosine (C) is similarly linked to guanine (G) (Fig. 12). This explains why the DNA of most organisms contains an equal number of A and T nucleotides, as well as G and C nucleotides.

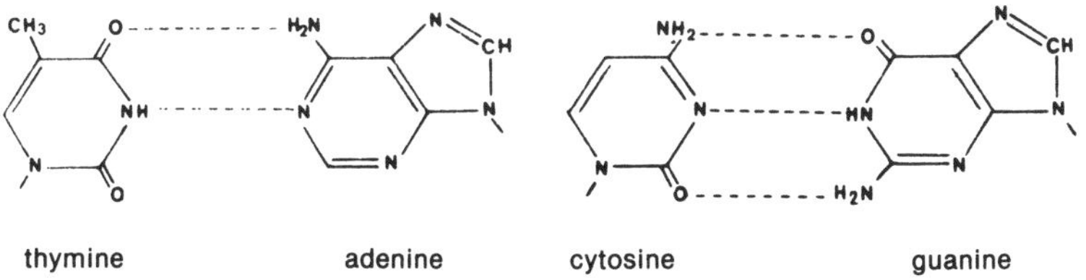

thymine   adenine   cytosine   guanine

Figure 12. Pairing by hydrogen-bonding of adenine and thymine, guanine and cytosine of DNA. In RNA adenine is bonded to uracil rather than thymine.

Besides hydrogen bonds, the helix is also held together by hydrophobic forces which act between the bases themselves. The amount of DNA per cell and the proportions of the four bases is characteristic of the species. Amino acids are reported to occur in the DNA of human leuco-

4. Philco, L., Blair, D. G., Tyler, A., and Vinograd, J. (1968) *Proc. Natl. Acad. Sci.* (Wash.), 59, 838.

cytes, spermatozoa, calf thymus cells, and vaccinia viruses.[5] Histones, a class of basic proteins present in the nuclei of diploid eukaryotic cells, bind to DNA and are thought to control the amount of information that can be expressed. The role of polyamines is currently being investigated.[6]

Ribonucleic acids are found as messenger (mRNA), ribosomal (rRNA), and transfer (tRNA) RNAs. Lesser degrees of base-pairing are seen among the RNAs. At those areas where there is hydrogen-bonding the strand of RNA may be folded back upon itself. The conformation of rRNA and tRNA is due to the peculiar manner in which RNA folds.[7] The primary nucleotide sequence of bacteriophage MS2 RNA has been established.[8] The polynucleotide chain is 3569 residues long. This is a significant technical achievement because the MS2 is "the first living organism for which the entire primary chemical structure has been elucidated." The secondary structure has been tentatively compared to a "bouquet" on account of the many radiating folds.

THE CHEMICAL SYNTHESIS OF POLYNUCLEOTIDES

Metaphosphate esters (MPE) will phosphorylate and condense nucleosides or, better still, nucleotides, to polynucleotides of about 10,000 in molecular weight, provided that the concentration of the monomers is kept at

---

5. Herskowitz, I. H. (1973) *Principles of Molecular Genetics*. Macmillan. New York. 3rd ed.
6. *Polyamines in Normal and Neoplastic Growth*. Russell, D. H. (ed.) Raven Press, Publishers. New York. 1973.
7. Levitt, M. (1969) *Nature,* 224, 759.
8. Fiers, W., Contreras, R., Dvernick, F., Haegeman, G., Iserentant, D., Merregaert, J., Min Jo, W., Molemans, F., Raeymaekers, A., Van den Berghe, A., Volckaert, G., and Ysebaert, M. (1976) *Nature,* 260, 500.

high as possible.[9,10] What is desirable is the forging of phosphate links between the 3'C and the 5'C of the pentoses, as in the natural polynucleotides. There should also be a minimum of side reactions giving rise to branching on the polymer. Schramm found that in his experiments with deoxyribonucleotides, pyrophosphate linkages were formed instead of the natural 3'-5' phosphate linkages.[9] Polyribonucleotides prepared from commercially available mixtures of 2' and 3' nucleoside phosphates yielded polymers that enzymatic digestion with snake venom phosphodiesterase and ribonuclease revealed to be poor in 3'-5' linkages. Kochetkov and his colleagues found "unequivocal evidence of favour of the predominance of the non-natural type of linkages" in their synthetic polyribonucleotides.[10] This has been the experience of other workers.[11]

The most successful strategy for polynucleotide synthesis is that of Khorana.[12] Oligonucleotides are synthesised first by a stepwise procedure. This procedure uses suitably protected deoxy-5'-mononucleotides and 3'-mononucleotides. The blocks of oligonucleotides are then condensed to polynucleotides. These elegant procedures would not be relevant for the abiotic random type of chemical reactions we are considering, but an indication of their power is seen in the recent synthesis of the double-stranded DNA molecule, 126 nucleotide pairs long, coding for $tRNA_1^{tyr}$ from E. coli.[13]

9. Schramm, G. (1965) in *The Origin of Prebiological Systems.* Fox, S. W. (ed.) Academic Press. p. 299.

10. Kochetkov, N. K., Budowsky, E. I., Domkin, V. D., and Khromov-Borissov, N. N. (1964) *Biochim. Biophys. Acta,* 80,145.

11. Hayes, F. N. and Hansbury, E. (1964) *J. Am. Chem. Soc.* 86, 4172.

12. Khorana, H. G. (1968) *Pure Appl. Chem.* 17, 349.

13. *J. Biol. Chem.* 251, 565-694. (1976).

EXPERIMENTS ON THE SELF-REPLICATION
OF POLYNUCLEOTIDES

The basic difficulty just outlined has not dampened enthusiasm in constructing theories as to how the primitive gene, once it arose, ensured its own replication. An interesting effect was noted by Schramm and his colleagues in the chemical polymerisation of polyuridylic acid (poly-U).[14] They found that the addition of polyadenylic acid increased the rate of polymerisation of poly-U by ten-fold. This slowed down when 20 - 30% of the uridylic acid was polymerised. One reason that has been offered is that the newly formed poly-U did not separate easily from the poly-A template.[9] Naylor's elegant studies[15] on some interactions and reactions of oligonucleotides in aqueous solutions have been quoted as another example of "hi-fi" nucleic acid replication without the benefit of enzymes.[16,17] Water soluble carbodiimides were used to activate terminal phosphate groups of oligonucleotides. Complex formation between these oligonucleotides and polyadenylic acid oriented the former so that thymidine penta- and hexanucleotides could be converted to thymidine deca- and dodecanucleotides respectively. The reaction mixtures required cooling to $-3°C$ over four days and the yield of the longer chains was less than 5%. Orgel has noted that while adenylic acid derivatives condense on a poly-U template, the converse reaction does not necessarily take place, probably because pyrimidine nucleotides do not stack well.[18]

The experiments described point to a tenuous possibility by which nucleic acids could have propagated themselves, but they do not suggest a way by which informa-

---

14. Schramm, G., Grotsch, H., and Pollman, W. (1961) *Angew. Chem.*, 73, 619.
15. Naylor, R. and Gilham, P. H. (1966) *Biochemistry*, 5, 2722.
16. Calvin, M. (1969) *Proc. Roy. Soc. Edinburgh.* Series B., 70, 273.
17. Calvin, M. (1969) *Chemical Evolution.* Clarendon Press. Oxford.
18. Orgel, L. E. (1968) *J. Mol. Biol.* 38, 381.

tional nucleic acids arose. Schramm has commented, "I wonder, however, whether a definite sequence of nucleotides can be selected by this mechanism and whether a higher amount of information accumulates in the nucleotide chains."[19]

THE ORIGIN OF THE GENETIC CODE

It was essential that primitive enzymes and other biologically important polypeptides be reproduced in some quantity for life to emerge. Could this have happened without the aid of nucleic acids? Some evidence for non-randomness in polypeptide elongation has been used to bolster this concept (p. 94). Orgel considered this possibility and concluded, "If the restrictions on nearest neighbours are weak, then no order is maintained for more than a few residues; if they are strong the variety of polypeptides which are formed is strictly limited, for once a few residues are connected together the rest of the sequence is determined. Thus we see that such a system is incapable of evolving by making a few discrete changes in the sequence of otherwise fully determined chains; all that can happen is that the whole pattern of nearest neighbour probabilities may change and so cause complicated changes in the distribution of all polypeptides in the system."[18] The reproduction of proteins, therefore, required coupling with an informational system involving nucleic acids, with the information stored and transmitted in the form of a code.

The origin of the genetic code remains a major problem in the coding field. The discussions ranging round this problem are fairly extensive; hypotheses are not wanting but, for different reasons, do not satisfactorily explain all the known facts.

The code is a linear sequence of nucleotide bases which specify each of the twenty amino acids. It is a triplet,

---

19. Ref. 9, p. 307.

allowing 4^3 or 64 triplets, which is ample for what is needed. Certain triplets are for punctuation, that is, they are signals for beginning and ending the synthesis of a polypeptide. There is no special punctuation between codons and the triplets do not overlap.[20] The code is also degenerate in that several triplets may code for the same amino acid. In such cases, generally it is in the third base that such triplets differ. The accepted codon assignments are based mainly on work with the E. coli cell-free system. As knowledge of the code has come from experiments with mRNA rather than DNA the term "code" really describes an RNA sequence. With certain exceptions it appears to be remarkably universal, such that poly-U always stimulates phenylalanine incorporation in cell-free systems, including those of algae, rat liver, and normal or malignant human cells. The exceptions lie in details of punctuation, number and location of repetitive sequences, and the reading of nonsense codons which vary between species.

The flow of information from DNA to protein is set out in a simplified form in Fig. 13.

In considering the origin of a primitive code, two important general points must be made. The first is that one cannot discuss the origin of the code without discussing the origin of the mechanism of protein synthesis. This has been observed by both Crick[23] and Woese.[24] The latter also noted that most hypotheses concerned with the origin of the code have tended to ignore the evolution of the translation mechanism. This primitive mechanism appears to have possessed an ancestor of tRNA,[18,24] or both tRNA and ribosomal RNA.[23] Possibly the primitive tRNA had a cavity which accommodated the distinctive side-chains of amino acids and, by aligning the acids, was

---

20. There is a recent report of a gene from the virus $\phi \times 174$ which can be read in two different ways to produce two entirely different proteins. Lewin, R. (1976). New Sci. 72, 148.

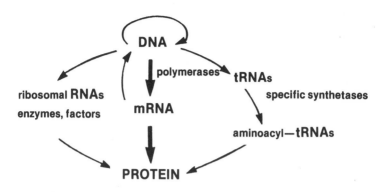

Figure 13. Simplified scheme of the flow of information in protein biosynthesis. The bold arrows mark the flow via mRNA specifying the primary sequence of the protein. The DNA, which replicates itself by a polymerase, also codes for the synthesis of ribosomal and tRNA. There is a flow of information from RNA to DNA at some stage in cells infected by oncogenic RNA viruses and even in normal mouse and human cells.[21] It is interesting to note that on the basis of information theory a mechanism of information flow from protein to nucleic acids is possible but it does not mean that it occurs.[22]

able to forge the peptide bonds. This means that the primitive tRNA had enzymatic properties and could utilize ATP or an alternative high-energy source. It should not be too difficult to look for catalytic activity among polynucleotides. At present there is no evidence for this.[25] A suggestion has been made that the primitive code's

21. Temin, H. M. and Mizutani, S. (1970) *Nature,* 226, 1211. Scolnick, E. M., Aaronson, S. A., Todaro, C. J., and Parks, W. P. (1971) *Nature,* 229, 318.
22. Ebringer, A. (1975) *J. Theoret. Biol.* 53, 243.
23. Crick, F. H. C. (1968) *J. Mol. Biol.* 38, 367.
24. Woese, C. R. (1969) in *Progress in Molecular and Subcellular Biology.* Hahn, F. E., Puck, T. T., Springer, G. F., and Wallenfels, K. (eds.) Springer-Verlag, Vol. 1, p. 1.
25. Ref. 18, p. 387.

recognition molecule was protein, not tRNA, but that this gave way to the latter in the interest of greater flexibility to the code's development.[26] A cycle has been proposed in which a protein-nucleotide complex promotes the replication of a polynucleotide which in turn promotes the synthesis of the same protein.[27]

The second point concerns the Principle of Continuity which must not be violated.[23] The code is universal and argues for a common ancestry of all organisms. Once established any change in it would have been lethal. The original code must have been a triplet code (though not all the three bases need be read) because a change in codon size necessarily makes nonsense of all previous messages.

How did the code come to possess the features that it has today? Why should there be just one set of codon assignments (one dictionary, as it were)? The many cell lines arising and evolving in various ecological niches would be expected to produce equally optimal assignments. It has been suggested that the primitive code was capable of specifying a few amino acids that were abundant (e.g. glycine, serine, alanine, aspartic acids) or, at any rate, specified for **classes** of amino acids (hydrophobic, charged, or with structural similarities). We may wonder at this juncture just what functionally useful molecules could possibly issue from a limited set of amino acids. However, according to Crick, the few amino acids allowed the operation of a simplified code employing adenine and inosine (A, I).[23] As Crick himself noted, if only the first two bases of the triplet were originally read the number of amino acids that could be coded was only four. The next step was the incorporation of the spatially smaller pyrimidines, uracil, and cytosine (U, C), or their

---

26. Caskey, C. T. (1970) *Quart. Rev. Biophys.*, 3, 295.
27. Chernavskii, D. S. and Chernavskaya, N. M. (1975) *J. Theoret. Biol.* 50, 13.

precursors, into the polynucleotide chain. This was brought about by a crucial "change in the replicase." As to why there are only four bases, Crick argues that these are stereochemically compatible in eventually forming the double helix. There are really two considerations here; suitability of various bases to act as code and their ability to form the double helix. Were the two of equal importance when the code first began to organise itself? Were there other bases which could code as well, but whose sequences were eliminated because they formed the double helix less satisfactorily? The reasoning becomes difficult to follow when the further evolution of the code is considered. Basically, we have a primitive protein enzyme which could ill afford being imperfectly replicated, partly because there was a paucity of equivalent amino acids which could be used interchangeably. An imprecise replicating system would have been valueless. Yet such a system is crucial to Crick's and Woese's hypotheses of the code's further development. Crick, for instance, argues that "the most likely step was that these primitive amino acids spread all over the code until almost all the triplets represented one or other of them."[28] As new amino acids arose they were also recognised by the codons already existing for similarly structured acids. Eventually codons acquired greater specificity. This could be one reason why, in the present code, similar amino acids tend to have similar codons. According to Woese, "the level of 'errors' in such a cell is so high that altering a codon assignment does little to worsen an already chaotic situation."[29] It is indeed a marvel that the primitive cell not only survived this, but propagated itself as well!

Woese has proposed a model (called the "TE" model,

28. Ref. 23, p. 374.
29. Ref. 24, p. 32.

for translation error) to explain the evolution of the code.[24] The translation apparatus of the primitive cell is supposed to have operated with a great deal of error. The deleterious effects of these errors were diluted by a continual reshuffling of codon assignments. A group of codons that differed only in the third position was assigned to the same amino acid. Assuming, on the basis of present knowledge of the code, that the first position of the triplet was less error-prone than the other two, Woese conjectures that those amino acids most essential to protein function would be related through the first position. As the translation mechanism of the cell improved in precision, changes in codon assignments became more damaging to the cell. Only those cells less prone to such changes survived; the set of codon assignments became "locked in," though more than one dictionary could survive under this hypothesis. The universality of the code lies then in the stereochemical necessity, that is, an amino acid must team up with only certain triplets. Woese directs attention to those features of today's code which support his model. Among these are the ambiguity of the base in the third position of a codon and the special features of the codons of "related" and "functional" amino acids.

But there are more than a few exceptions to the rule and a number of "in-betweens" which render Woese's model no more valid than the others. For instance, leucine, phenylalanine, and proline have functional importance in protein structure and they do not have purine-rich codons, nor is a purine found in the second position of their codons. Tyrosine may be obtained from phenylalanine by hydroxylation, yet it has a purine in its codon's second position. Of the six serine codons, none is purine-rich, and only two have guanine in position two. The features said to characterise "related" amino acids also do not bear close scrutiny because of the impossibility of defining, within reasonable limits, what "related" means in the context of protein functions. Attempts to show that the "relatedness" stems from a direct amino acid-nucleotide relationship have not ben successful.[30,31] In any case, an inspection of the dictionary does not reveal that there is a single type of codon which is unique for a given amino acid. This does not preclude the importance of a physical interaction between amino acids and polynucleotides at some stage of the code's origin,[18,23,24,32,33] perhaps through photochemical reactions.[34] These primitive amino acid-nucleotide pairing experiments by Nature suffer from another difficulty. The amino acids attached to the anticodon trinucleotides (proto t-RNA) would be held far apart when they pair subsequently with a polynucleotide template. It is unlikely that they could condense together efficiently.[35]

The main features of the modern code can be explained by Woese's model with special pleading. The logical necessity of having an inaccurate primitive translation system obtains in both Crick's and Woese's models. How would such a system confer a selective functional advantage on a cell? Orgel tries to work out a development of the code in two phases. In the first, natural selection without function, there is assumed a phase of fairly accurate non-enzymatic template synthesis of polynucleotides. Certain of these sequences were selected over against others by reason of their possessing enzymatic activities, such as producing activated precursors, replication, and hydrolysis. This phase is followed by the formation of stereospecific complexes between amino acids and the functional self-reproducing polynucleotides. Polypeptides acting as activating enzymes arose, which on being

---

30. Steinman, G. and Cole, M. N. (1967) *Proc. Natl. Acad. Sci.* (Wash.). 58, 737.
31. Welton and Woese (unpublished results, quoted in Ref. 24, p. 36).
32. Woese, C. R. (1968) *Proc. Natl. Acad. Sci.* (Wash.). 59, 110.
33. Lacey, J. C. and Pruitt, K. M. (1969) *Nature,* 233, 799.
34. Lesk, A. M. (1970) *J. Theor. Biol.,* 27, 171.
35. *The Origins of Life on the Earth.* Miller, S. L. and Orgel, L. E. Prentice-Hall, Inc., Englewood Cliffs, New Jersey. (1974) p. 163.

improved upon by a process of mutation and selection, became fairly specific for their amino acids. A complex genetic code then evolved.

It has been shown on models that the polymer structure of α-helical polylysine was conducive to the complementary stacking of 5' adenosine monophosphate (with ribose as the sugar) and in predicting GGG as a glycine codon.[33] Part of the propensity for nucleotide to stack on nucleotide is due, in the model, to the interaction of 2'-OH of one nucleotide with the phosphoryl oxygen of its neighbour. As deoxyribonucleotides do not have a 2'-OH this suggests to the authors that RNA evolved before DNA. But natural RNA is linked by 5'3' and not the 5'2' internucleotide bonds that the model depicts. This is no argument, of course, against the possibility of a primitive RNA having the latter type of linkage though that possibility is a remote one. In addition to the objection of an unnatural linkage is the experimental fact that natural RNAs (with 5' 3' bonds) do form both soluble and insoluble complexes with polylysine.[36] A model for these complexes was proposed and discussed which involved an extended collinear complex of RNA and polylysine, in which one was coiled around the other so that corresponding phosphates and ϵ-amino groups were close to one another. Thus the model of Lacey and Pruitt is inconclusive with regard to the primacy of RNA and its role in the origin of the genetic code. Recently it has been shown that in a solvent of 80% acetone - 20% water, lysine complexed to polyadenylic acid will form dilysine to the extent of 2.6%.[37] The coupling agent is 1,3-bis-(2-methoxyethyl) carbodiimide. Without polyadenylic acid the yield was 0.8%. Since AAA

---

36. Sober, H. A., Schlossman, S. F., Yaron, A., Latt, S. A., and Rushizky, G. W. (1966) *Biochemistry*, 5, 3608.
37. Bjornson, L. K., Lemmon, R. M., and Calvin, M. (1974) in *The Origin of Life and Evolutionary Biochemistry*. Dose, K., Fox, S. W., Deborin, G. A., and Pavlovskaya, T. E. (eds.) Plenum Press. New York and London. p. 21.

is a codon for lysine these results are taken to support the concept (Woese's really) that the polynucleotide played a role in the chemical evolution of the polypeptides. Apart from demonstrating the very special conditions under which dilysine is formed, what is the purpose of the experiment? It is clear already that when the dielectric constant is lowered with acetone there is maximum ionic binding between lysine and the polynucleotide. Supposing it can be shown that no other basic amino acid could be induced to complex in a similar fashion; it no more proves that the codon for lysine was so derived evolutionarily than it can disprove that AAA was rejected as a codon for some other acid.

As an aside, it is noteworthy that the model building carries its own peculiar snares. Woese and his co-workers[38] using trinucleotide models found that a greater number of amino acids could be induced to make a "good fit" than was reported by another group of workers.[39] Crick has also reported that he has found errors in some models.[40]

On the chemical front Calvin and his associates have discovered that adenine on a solid support accepted glycine better than phenylalanine. They were attempting to elucidate the kind of selectivity operating at the -C-C-A end of the tRNAs, believing that this triplet is a residue of some prebiological significance.[16]

CONCLUSION

The foregoing survey of a few theories on the origin of the genetic code has highlighted the formidable difficulties that face investigators in this field. The initial excitement over the unravelling of the code has given·way to

---

38. Woese, C. R., Dugre, D. H., Dugre, S. A., Kondo, M., and Saxinger, W. C. (1966) *Cold Spring Harbour Symposium in Quantitative Biology*, 31, 723.
39. (a) Pelc, S. R. and Welton, M. G. E. (1966) *Nature*, 209, 868.
    (b) Welton, M. G. E. and Pelc, S. R. (1966) *Nature*, 209, 870.
40. Crick, F. H. C. (1967) *Nature*, 213, 798.

a more sober assessment of the evolutionary problems. The critical experiments have yet to be done and much remains to be known in the control of protein biosynthesis before the problem of origin can be defined.

Yĉas closed his lucid exposition on the evolution of the code[41] by quoting Crick, whose verdict on the matter in the present state can hardly be bettered. "In the last years there has been a rash of papers on its structure and origin. . . . The point I want to emphasise here is that we may be heading for a very unhealthy situation, in that theory will run far ahead of useful experimental facts . . . . I hope, therefore, that when people put forward detailed theories about the origin of the genetic code, they will try if possible to produce ones which can be tested in some way or other."

For the sake of completeness, we must mention that there are investigators who feel that the nucleic acid-based genetic mechanism was a late arrival on the evolutionary scene, rather than being itself part of the most primitive living system.[42-46]

41. Yĉas, M. (1969) The Biological Code. North-Holland Publishing Co. Vol. 12.
42. Eakin, R. E. (1963) Proc. Natl. Acad. Sci. (Wash.) 49, 360.
43. Lipmann, F. (1965) Ref. 9, p. 259.
44. Hanson, E. D. (1966) Quart. Rev. Biol., 41, 1.
45. Allen, G. (1970) Perspect. Biol. and Med., 14, 109.
46. Kritskii, M. S. (1975) International Seminar on "The Origin of Life." Biology Bulletin of the Academy of Sciences of the USSR. (Translated from Russian.) Consultants Bureau. 2, 149.

Chapter 4

The Origin of Enzymes

INTRODUCTION

This section deals with the structure and function of an important class of macromolecules—the proteins which have catalytic activity. Several texts can be consulted for greater coverage and detail, some of which are listed below. [1,2,6] Here we are attempting a short survey as we pass from a consideration of the abiotic synthesis of biologically important monomers to an examination of how their functional polymers might have arisen. Can we plausibly affirm that such enzyme polymers would have evolved predestined, as it were, from their monomeric units? We cannot, of course, expect that the primitive molecules were wholly like their modern counterparts. This proviso gives leeway to the operation of selection pressures over aeons of time.

The answer to the question may be approached at two levels. This is not merely a heuristic device. Investigations of the problem of origins seem to fall into one or another of the two categories.

a. An examination of the factors which could have contributed to the origin of functional proteins, such as enzymes.

b. The detection of evolutionary relationships among

---

1. Barry, J. M. and Barry, E. M. (1969) *An Introduction to the Structure of Biological Molecules.* Prentice-Hall, Inc. Englewood Cliffs, New Jersey.

2. Haschemeyer, R. H. and Haschemeyer, A. E. V. (1973) *Proteins, a guide to study by physical and chemical methods.* Wiley & Sons, Inc. New York.

3. Jirgensons, B. and Hnilca, L. S. (1965) *Biochim. Biophys. Acta* 109, 241.

4. Campbell, P. N. (1965) in *Progress in Biophysics and Molecular Biology.* Butler, J. A. V. and Noble, D. (eds.) Pergamon Press, Vol. 15, p. 1.

5. *The Mechanism of Protein Synthesis.* Cold Spring Harbour Symposia in Quantitative Biology. 1969. Vol. 35.

6. *Macromolecules, Biosynthesis, and Function.* Ochoa, S., Asensio, C., Heredia, C. F. and Nachmansohn, D. (eds.) Academic Press. (1970).

certain proteins by testing for homology. That is, a similarity in the sequence of amino acids of two proteins may be due to their possessing a common ancestral gene. This is dealt with in the following chapter.

The first approach works forward in time from an assumed set of primeval conditions, while the second attempts to reconstruct a dynamic sequence of events to account for amino acid sequences in their present-day forms.

PROTEINS

Structure

Proteins consist of chains of amino acids linked by peptide bonds between amino and carboxyl groups. As commonly used, the term polypeptide refers to proteins of M.W. 5000 or less, though it is obvious that some ambiguity will occur. Proteins have several levels of structural complexity—helices, pleated forms, polypeptide chains folded into units, and subunits united into larger and more complex quarternary structures.

The peptide bond is the main covalent link in chain formation. Another covalent bond, the disulphide, usually contributes to the formation of the tertiary structure. Weaker bonds, such as hydrogen, ionic, and non-polar hydrophobic bonds participate, in number varying from protein to protein, at secondary and higher levels of organisation of the molecule. Proteins fold in a manner that the amino acids bearing the non-polar side chains are inside and most of those acids with polar groups are outside the folded unit. The environment also affects protein conformation. Thus histones which are highly extended in pure water because of their high content of basic amino acids (lysine, arginine) are folded up at sufficiently high concentrations of electrolytes, for example, at DNA chains containing ionised phosphate.[3]

The formation of a dipeptide is accompanied by an increase of free energy of about 3 kcal/mol with the reactants at molar concentrations. The equilibrium constant is

$$K = e^{-3,000/RT} = e^{-5} \simeq 0.01$$

The reaction will tend to be in the direction of the hydrolysis of the dipeptide rather than its synthesis. The energy requirements for protein biosynthesis is met by the hydrolysis of high-energy phosphate bonds of GTP and ATP. At least three of these bonds are utilised for the formation of each peptide bond. The total biosynthetic process has been worked out in especially great detail for E. Coli and reticulocytes.[4,5]

Protein Biosynthesis

The genetic information of a section of the DNA in the nucleus is duplicated on a strand of messenger RNA (mRNA). This is transcription and involves an enzyme, DNA-dependent RNA polymerase.

One of the great accomplishments of recent years is the solving of the genetic code, that is, the relationship of nucleotide sequence to amino acid sequence. This point has been elaborated in the discussion on the genesis of the primitive gene. It is now well known that the code for a single amino acid (a codon) consists of a nucleotide triplet. For instance three uridylic monophosphate units occurring in sequence, UUU, is the signal for the amino acid phenylalanine to be incorporated. A polypeptide containing 146 amino acids would be coded by an mRNA of about 450 for beginning and terminating synthesis, as well as signals separating nucleotide sequences coding for an entire protein (a cistron) from those coding for next protein, [6,7]

Transfer of mRNA to the cytoplasm, presumably via

7. *Polymerisation in Biological Systems.* Ciba Foundation Symposium 7. Elsevier. *Excerpta Medica.* North-Holland. Associated Scientific Publishers. (1972).

pores in the nuclear membrane, is followed by the process of translation and polypeptide formation. This takes place on the surface of specialised microstructures called ribosomes.

A ribosome consists of two dissociable 30 and 70 S pieces. The complete ribosome undergoes conformational changes requiring energy which is supplied by the hydrolysis of GTP. The details of the mechanism differ somewhat in microorganisms and in animals and, no doubt, much remains to be elucidated about these differences. What is known, however, is that besides mRNA, ribosomal RNAs, over 40 specific tRNAs and GTP, ATP, and Mg^{2+} are essential. At least 100 protein molecules are associated with the process. These include 20 aminoacyl tRNA synthetases, the 5b proteins of the ribosome, and a dozen protein factors involved in the different functions of the ribosome.

It is well known that in prokaryotes protein synthesis is started with N-formyl methionine, the formyl groups of which is later removed. There is evidence that the C terminal of the nascent polypeptide chain requires the action of a proteolytic enzyme to "mature" the product.[8] From all appearances protein biosynthesis is a complicated and well-integrated multi-component mechanism which ensures that the product is a correct interpretation in amino acid "language" of the corresponding nucleotide code present in the DNA. Such a masterpiece of sophistication has been attributed to the ingenuity of the evolutionary process. But as further work brings to light even finer details of its control and regulation, it becomes more and more evident that there is a need to evolve a satisfactory explanation as well.

GLYCOPROTEINS

These are fairly common and biologically important

---

8. Black, J. A., Stenzel, P. and Harkins, R. N. (1975) *J. Theor. Biol.* **50**, 161.

proteins. They have short chains of sugars attached to them through the amide and hydroxyl functions of asparagine and serine, threonine, respectively. Among them are enzymes, antibodies, hormones, transport proteins, and proteins involved in clot formation. They have characteristic sugar components which include D-glucose, D-galactose, D-mannose, L-fucose, D-xylose, L-arabinose, and their acetylated amino derivatives.[9]

The attachment of carbohydrate to the protein takes place at the membranes of the endoplasmic reticulum. Here a series of glycosyltransferases transfers activated sugars from their nucleotide derivatives to the appropriate receptors on the protein molecule. These transferases must act in concert in order to assemble the correct sequence of sugar units. The regulation of glycoprotein synthesis is under current investigation. It is now clear that one of the pathways of the synthesis of glycoproteins involves the prior assembly of at least a portion of the oligosaccharide chain while it is attached to the lipid, dolichol phosphate.[10]

What correlation is there of carbohydrate with the function of the glycoprotein? The information on this is limited. The activities of chorionic gonadotrophin and follicle stimulating hormone are lost upon removal of the terminal sialic acid residues of their carbohydrate moieties. A marked drop in viscosity of the mucins results from a similar treatment. Yet the transport function of a number of plasma proteins is unaffected. Carbohydrate is found on the Fc portions of the heavy chains of IgG, associated with certain biological activities such as complement fixation, placental transfer, and cytophilicity. A regulatory function can also be discerned. For example, the cleavage of the terminal sialic acid residues of

9. *Glycoproteins.* Gottschalk, A. (ed.) Elsevier, Amsterdam. (1972) 2nd edition.
10. Lennarz, W. J. (1975) *Science,* 188, 986.

caeruloplasmin acts as a signal for the liver to remove the protein from the circulation.[11]

What is known for a very limited number of glycoproteins already demonstrates the diversity of structure of the carbohydrate units and implicates their participation in biological activity. In some cases the carbohydrate is indispensable for activity. For these molecules anyway the further implication is that unless the biosynthetic apparatus for protein and carbohydrate evolved pari passu and intercalated at some point in time it would not have been possible for them to have existed and/or functioned. This remark applies as well to other complex proteins such as lipoproteins.

ENZYMES

The existence of enzymes is essential for life since the most important functions of organisms are carried out by them.[12] Although enzymes cannot synthesise themselves directly they are linked to the synthesis of nucleic acids, which in turn code for their, and much of the cell's structures. It is interesting to observe that the origin of the enzymes acts as a watershed in any discussion of the origin of life. It serves to divide the speculative fancies, erected upon the experimental production of the racemic mixtures of amino acids, from the reality that these monomers could not have, as easily as we are led to believe, come together to form anything resembling the simplest enzyme of a "primitive" organism living today.

Theories on the Origin of Enzymes

Keosian thinks that the absorption of catalysts on colloids, especially proteins, will lead to the formation of

---

11. Ashwell, G. and Morell, A. (1974) in *The Metabolism and Function of Glycoproteins.* Smellie, R. M. S. and Beeley, J. G. (eds.) Biochemical Society Symposium No. 40. London: The Biochemical Society. p. 177.
12. *Enzymes.* Dixon, M. and Webb, E. C. Longmans, (1964) 2nd edition. p. 665.

metalloorganic catalysts, and eventually, enzymes.[13] In a similar vein Bernal believes that complexes of the commoner transition elements (iron, copper, manganese, cobalt) acting as inorganic catalysts were successfully modified by coordination with the porphyrins. "From these, such universally active enzymes as catalase and cytochrome must have been formed. Some such primitive enzymes may subsequently have lost their original metal centre, modifying thereby, but not losing their catalytic characater."[14] Explanations of this sort are facile beyond the limits allowed by certain known properties of metalloprotein enzymes. The metal ions do not normally appreciably dissociate, that is, they are not in reversible equilibrium with the free metal ions in solution. In any case the loss of the metal ion will deprive the enzyme of its catalytic activity. How the proposed modification came about therefore is hard to see.

The literature is generously endowed with ideas about the existence of "proto-enzymes" and "proto-coenzymes." An example is a recommendation made by Dayhoff and her colleagues. "In the absence of a suitable, more general word, we hope that 'enzyme' will be extended in usage to include catalytic nucleic acid molecules. Such a general concept is needed in evolutionary studies to include the more primitive stages of biochemical systems. There must have been 'proto-enzymes' which were much smaller, much less efficient and much less specific than those today."[15] This article of faith seems acceptable, if only because it employs an argument by analogy. In biology we recognise a gradation in

---

13. *The Origin of Life.* Keosian, J. Chapman and Hall Ltd. London (1964) p. 27.
14. *The Origin of Life.* Bernal, J. D. Weidenfeld and Nicholson. London. (1967) p. 62.
15. Dayhoff, M. O. in *Atlas of Protein Sequence and Structure* (1969) Dayhoff, M. O. (ed.) National Biomedical Research Foundation. Vol. 4, p. 107.

structure of living things from the simple unicellular organism to the most complex metazoa. We are dealing, however, with molecules whose functions, we are told, might have been served, though less efficiently, by molecules not related to proteins. This is an attempt to bridge a gap that looks more like a chasm. One suspects that proposals of this sort stem from a lack of appreciation of the properties and the role of enzymes. It is true that they contain the same kind of amino acids as found in other proteins, but they form a unique class because of their characteristics.

a. They lower the energy barrier of activation and accelerate the approach of a chemical reaction to an equilibrium.
b. They allow catalysis of closely related compounds, that is, enzymes have a high specificity for their substrates.
c. They can form "multi-enzyme" systems.
d. They differ from simple catalysts in that their very structure makes possible a fine control of metabolic processes, for instance, via allosteric binding sites.

Some compounds, individually or in series, may show one or two of the features outlined. A case in point is the remarkable decomposition of nucleoside diphosphate sugars catalysed by metal ions. Among the sugar phosphates tested uridine diphosphate glucose (UDPGlc) and uridine diphosphate galactose (UDPGal) possess pyranose rings with equatorial 2-OH groups. These enabled the formation of 5-membered 1,2 cyclic phosphates, liberating uridine monophosphate (UMP). This catalytic breakdown by metals was not seen with uridine diphosphate N-acetylglucosamine, guanosine diphosphate mannose, and guanosine diphosphate fucose.[16] Some sort of specificity is thus evident. Protein enzymes alone combine at least the first three and, frequently, all four of the properties in order to perform the orderly, sequential ar-

---

16. Nunez, H. A. and Barker, R. (1976) *Biochemistry*, 15, 3843.

ray of chemical reactions which we recognise as the hallmark of the metabolising organism. It is this resultant flexible integration within the economy of the organism that allows selection pressure to operate.

The Origin of Catalytic Proteins

This problem may be approached from two directions. One may argue for the possibility of a polymer possessing weak catalytic function arising by sheer chance out of the enormous numbers of amino acid polymers that could theoretically have been formed. Agents aiding the process of polymerisation undoubtedly were present. But Dixon and Webb have convincingly demonstrated the unlikelihood of such an event.[12] Oparin is in agreement with this. "Enzymes possess exceptional activity and specificity of catalytic action simply because their intra-molecular structure is perfectly adapted to the accomplishment of their biological function; but this adaptability, of course, cannot arise accidentally in a simple solution of organic compounds."[17] In any case, the scattered occurrence of catalysts in the primeval broth that were not able to replicate themselves could hardly serve as the basis for life to emerge.

The second approach is to look at the enzymes that we have today and try to determine how they really work. It may then be possible to find a few common denominators, among the active sites, for instance. Modern methods for sequencing the amino acids of proteins coupled with the results obtained from X-ray crystallography have emboldened this approach. Sufficiently complete definitions of structure, as well as a rigorous analysis of the mechanism of catalysis, are now available for a number of enzymes.[18,19]

---

17. *Genesis and Evolutionary Development of Life.* Oparin, A. I. Academic Press, (1968) p. 136.
18. *The Structure and Action of Proteins.* Dickerson, R. E. and Geis, I. Harper and Row. (1969).
19. *A Discussion on the Structure and Function of Proteolytic Enzymes.* Phil. Trans. Roy. Soc. Lond. Series B. 257, 63 (1970).

The Active Site

Model enzymes have been produced which bind the substrate in such a way that attack with well-placed functional groups can follow. Hydrophobic binding within a cyclodextrin cavity has been utilised.[20] Some success has also been reported for the non-protein simulation of nitrogenase reactions, as reviewed by Schrauzer.[21] The reduction of molecular nitrogen to ammonia by cyano complexes of Mo^{iv}, in the presence of ATP, has been unequivocally demonstrated. Further development of this work will be awaited with more than ordinary interest by virtue of the importance of nitrogen fixation. Schrauzer closes his review with a cautionary note. "Any attempt to develop systems which duplicate enzymes more closely or quantitatively would require a substantial increase of their complexity, eventually the partial synthesis of the enzyme itself."

The relatively few amino acids that actually perform the catalytic function of the enzyme is known as the active site. Apart from possibly yielding clues on the mechanism of catalysis, active sites have been the focus of interest from the viewpoint of phylogenetic classification. It is believed that the sequence of amino acids near the catalytic site is highly conserved, even in very distantly related proteins. Consequently, maps of active site peptides collected from various sources reflect the intense interest paid to this part of enzyme anatomy in recent years.[15] Table 3 lists a few of these peptides and their parent enzymes.

---

20. Breslow, R. (1971) in *Bioinorganic Chemistry*. Gould, R. F. (ed.) American Chemical Society Publications. p. 21.
21. Schrauzer, G. N. (1975) *Angew. Chemie, Internat. Edit.* 14, 514.

TABLE 3[22]

Enzyme	Active Peptide							
Chymotrypsin A (Bovine)	Met	Gly	Asp	<u>Ser</u>	Gly	Gly	Pro	Leu
Trypsin (Sheep)	Gln	Gly	Asp	<u>Ser</u>	Gly	Gly	Pro	Val
Yeast Alcohol Dehydrogenase	Thr	Gly	Ile	<u>Cys</u>	Arg	Ser	Asp	Asp
Trypsin (Bovine)	Ser	Ala	Ala	<u>His</u>	Cys	Tyr	Lys	Ser
Alkaline Phosphatase (E. Coli)	Val	Thr	Asp	<u>Ser</u>	Ala	Ala	Ser	Ala
Aldolase (Rabbit Muscle)	Thr	Leu	Leu	<u>Lys</u>	Asn	Pro	Met	Val

Alkaline phosphatase, trypsin, chymotrypsin, elastase, thrombin, and many other enzymes are serine proteases or esterases. They possess a very reactive serine at their active site (underscored in Table 3) but, of course, the positions are different for the different enzymes. The essential serine in chymotrypsin is Ser 195 and that for trypsin is Ser 183. The reagent diisopropyl fluorophosphate (DFP) specifically attaches to Ser 195 of bovine chymotrypsin even though there are 27 other serine residues in the molecule.

An understanding of the overall mechanism of catalysis has been derived not so much from the amino acid sequences of the active **peptide** as from the structure of the active **site**. Evidence for the importance of the active site comes from two quarters, which we will now discuss.

The implication of the imidazole group of histidine as essential to the activity of numerous hydrolytic enzymes has led to studies of the ability of imidazoles to catalyse

---

22. Ref. 15. p. 45-51

the hydrolysis of several substrates. These substances include thiol esters[23] and phenyl acetates.[23,24] The pentapeptide L-threonyl-L-alanyl-L-seryl-L-histidyl-L-aspartic acid has been synthesised and investigated as a catalyst for the hydrolysis of p-nitrophenyl acetate.[25] This pentapeptide had a catalytic activity six times greater than that reported for any other synthetic peptide in the hydrolysis of p-nitrophenyl acetate. Treatment of the peptide with DFP led to a 48% decrease in catalytic efficiency.[26] An unusual peptide, L-seryl-γ-aminobutyryl-L-histidyl-γ-aminobutyryl-L-aspartic acid was also synthesised.[26] This turned out to be an even more potent esterase model. Both the peptides exhibited some degree of stereoselectivity, with a preference for L-esters. Imidazole itself showed no preferences. The γ-aminobutyric acid residues were introduced to allow greater flexibility of the chain, and the almost threefold increase in catalytic power led the authors to believe that imidazole catalysis could not be the sole explanation. Other effects associated with the interaction of the amino acid chains might have been operative. In the same year Woolley synthesised a hexadecapeptide by the solid phase method. It showed no esterolytic activity toward acetylphenylalanine ethyl ester and no proteolytic activity against serum albumin.[27] These findings were indicative that, for specific chymotryptic activity, more was required than histidine and serine residues interspersed at frequent intervals along a peptide chain.

There is good reason, of course, for the relatively low activity of even a faithful reproduction of what cor-

23. Bender, M. L. and Turnquest, B. W. (1957) *J. Am. Chem. Soc.* 79, 1652, 1656.
24. Bruice, T. C. and Schmir, C. L. (1958) *J. Am. Chem. Soc.* 80, 148.
25. Cruickshank, P. and Sheehan, J. C. (1964) *J. Am. Chem. Soc.* 86, 2070.
26. Sheehan, J. C., and Bennet, G. B. and Schneider, J. A. (1966) *J. Am. Chem. Soc.* 88, 3455.
27. Woolley, D. W. (1966) *J. Am. Chem. Soc.* 88, 2309.

responds to the active peptide of an enzyme. The concluding remarks of M. F. Perutz following the discussion on the structures and functions of proteolytic enzymes are illuminating. We quote these remarks before examining in greater detail the experimental findings that prompted them. "The activation of the serine oxygen to a powerful nucleophile by the buried negative charge of the aspartic acid explains why certain analogues of the active site, constructed by organic chemists on what appeared to be reasonable assumptions, nevertheless had a catalytic activity lower than chymotrypsin by a factor of a thousand. These analogues contained the hydroxyl and imidazole groups in sterically favourable positions, but lacked the buried negative charge now seen to be required to activate them."[28]

THE ACTIVE SITE OF BOVINE CHYMOTRYPSIN

The amino acid sequence of bovine α-chymotrypsin was worked out by Hartley in 1964.[29] Before this event, the modification of several amino acid residues was found to destroy enzyme activity. These residues are now known.
a. Acylation of Ser 195
b. Photo-oxidation or alkylation of His 57
c. Acetylation of the amino group of Ile 16.

The creation of space-filling models of chymotrypsin (M.W. 24,500) following X-ray diffraction studies has highlighted the importance of the part played by the conformation of the polypeptide chain in the structure of the catalytic and binding sites. The enzyme molecule turns out to be roughly spherical with many segments of the chain folding upon itself in anti-parallel pleats, rather than forming α-helices.[30] α-helices are present from residues

28. Ref. 19, p. 265.
29. Hartley, B. S. (1964) Nature, 201, 1284.
30. Birktoft, J. J., Blow, D. M., Henderson, R., and Steitz, T. A. in Ref. 19, p. 67-76.

164-170 and 234-245. There are five disulphide bridges which are responsible for folding the entire molecule into a number of loops. The activation of bovine chymotrypsinogen is accompanied by the loss of two dipeptides, Ser 14-Arg 15, and Thr 147-Asn 148, creating 3 polypeptide chains, A, B, C thereby.

The catalytic site is formed by the convergence of His 57, Ser 195, and Asp 102. The site is adjacent to a hydrophobic area on the molecule, suitably shaped to accommodate a substrate molecule and orientate it in relation to the active centre. It is now possible to speculate on the molecular conformational changes which take place following the activation of bovine α-chymotrypsinogen and when, as chymotrypsin, it exercises its hydrolytic action on a suitable substrate.

One of the consequences of the loss of the dipeptide, Ser 14-Arg 15, is the creation of an α-amino group at Ile 16, which now becomes the amino terminal of the B chain. Being protonated, this group forms an internal ion pair with the negatively charged carboxyl group of Asp 194. Asp 194 swings out of the way and permits an apparently crucial spatial relation between the adjacent Ser 195 and His 57 at the active site of the enzyme (Fig. 14).

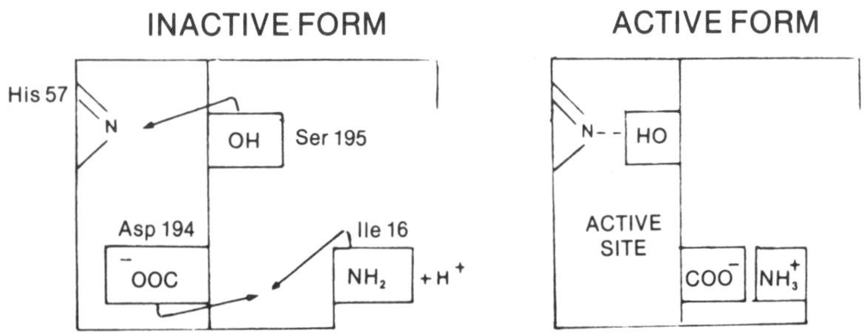

Figure 14. [After Hess, et al][31] The diagram represents a part of the chymotrypsin molecule and shows the movements of the amino acid residues concerned in order to obtain a functional conformation at the active site.

31. Hess, G. P., McConn, J., Ku, E. and McConkey, G. Ref. 19, p. 89-104.

The intercalation of His 57 between Asp 102, buried in the interior of the molecule, and Ser 195, opens the possibility of electron transfer by rearrangement of hydrogen bonds. This amounts to a "charge-relay system" in which the negative charge of the aspartate carboxyl is conveyed to the seryl oxygen (Fig. 15). Ser 195 becomes a strong nucleophile which is able to attack the carbonyl atom of the peptide bond that is to undergo scission.

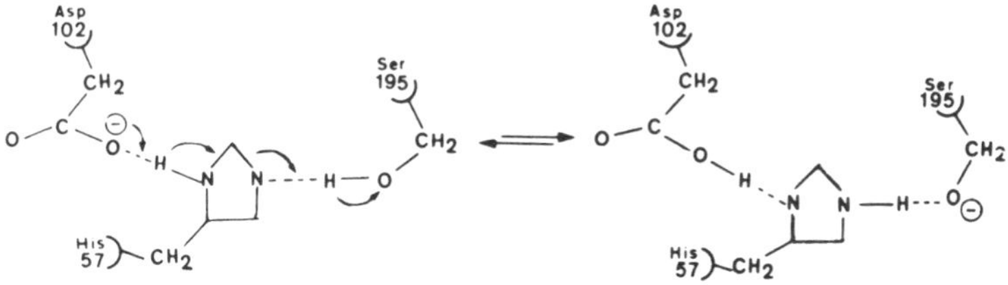

Figure 15. [After Birktoft, et al][30]

The hydrophobic binding site already referred to is made up of residues 184-191 and 214-227. In such an environment the side chains of phenylalanine, tryptophan, and tyrosine are attracted. This explains the preferential hydrolysis by chymotrypsin of peptide linkages involving the aromatic amino acids.

Only a small number of enzymes has been studied at the molecular level. From the findings that have accumulated thus far it would appear that for the enzymes elastase[32] and subtilisin BPN[33] serine, histidine, and a buried aspartic acid residue are similarly implicated at the catalytic site. The participation of amino acid residues from different segments of the polypeptide chain in bind-

---

32. Watson, H. C. and Shotton, D. M. (1969) Private communication. Ref. 18.
33. Wright, C. S., Alden, R. A. and Kraut, J. A.)1969) *Nature*, 221, 235.

ing the substrate has been found for carboxypeptidase[34] and the active sites of subtilisin[35] and papain.[36] Papain is a sulphydryl enzyme of 212 amino acid residues. The free SH groups of Cys 25, together with His 159, Asn 175, and Asp 158 are responsible for the splitting of the substrate. If the SH group is blocked by disulphide formation with cysteine or chelation by a metal ion proteolytic activity is lost.

Three dimensional models of ribonuclease S have shown the presence of His 12 and 19 and Lys 7 and 41 near the nucleotide binding sites. These residues have been shown by chemical studies to be essential for catalytic activity.[37] For egg white lysozyme the essential side chains for substrate binding and catalysis appear to be Asp 52, Trp 62, Trp 13, Asp 101, and Asp 103.[38] The high concentration of non-polar side chains at the active site of aldolase is noteworthy.[39] From kinetic studies there is also evidence of glucose mediating a change between conformational isomers of the enzyme glucose oxidase.[40]

Concerning the catalytic site, therefore, at least two important points have emerged from the discussion so far; namely, the absolute requirement of certain amino acid residues (for example, Ser 195 in chymotrypsin, Cys 25 in papain) and the composite nature of the site which makes mandatory the participation of certain key residues from different regions of the polypeptide chain. A definite, mobile mosaic of amino acid residues performs the func-

34. Lipscomb, W. N., Reeke, G. N., jun, Hartsuck, J. A., Quicho, F. A., and Bethge, P. H. (1970) Ref. 19, p. 231 - 236.
35. Alden, R. A., Wright, C. S., and Kraut, J. (1970) Ref. 19, p. 119-124.
36. Drenth, J., Jansonium, J. N., Keokoek, R., Sluyterman, L. A. A. and Wolthers, B. G. (1970) Ref. 19, p. 231-236.
37. Wyckoff, H. W., Hardman, K. D., Allewell, N. M., Ingami, T., Johnson, L. N. and Richards, F. M. (1967) J. Biol. CHem. 242, 3984.
38. A Discussion on the Structure and Function of Lysozyme. Proc. Roy. Soc. Lond. Series B. 167, 349-448 (1967). See also Ref. 19.
39. Morse, D. E. and Horecker, B. L. (1968) Adv. in Enzymol. 31, 125.
40. Duke, F. R., Weibel, M., Page, D. S., Bulgrin, V. G. and Luthy, J. (1969) J. Am. Chem. Soc. 91, 3904.

tion of catalysis and substrate binding. This means that the entire molecule, or most of it, is necessary. This appears to preclude an evolution from simpler structures. Take, for argument's sake, the sequence L-threonyl-L-alanyl-L-seryl-L-histidyl-L-aspartic acid. It was carefully synthesised with the foreknowledge that seryl and histidyl residues are involved in hydrolytic enzymes. A more propitious conglomeration of residues to imitate a proto-enzyme could hardly be imagined. It is doubtful whether the mechanism of preferred pairing of amino acids, thought to be operative in abiotic synthesis, could imaginably better the combination.[41] Some catalytic activity was noted for this sequence. However, as a peptide begins to lengthen there is no reason why it should retain its catalytic power. This seems to be the lesson of Woolley's experiment.[27] The hexadecapeptide chain* was, again, engineered to favour catalytic activity. The absence of activity in this case may mean that the right combination of amino acids was not hit upon. On the other hand, the conclusion may equally well be that the genesis of a proto-enzyme is not such a likely event after all. More experiments of this kind are clearly necessary. One can, for instance, build upon the active peptides of chymotrypsin and look for the minimum number of additions to the chain that will evince any degree of esterolytic activity. If these are not found, substitutions, such as one hydrophobic residue for another, could be tried.

Consider now the evolution, not of peptides into fully-fledged enzymes, but of, say, haemoglobin from myoglobin.[42] In order that the single protein chain of the latter should somehow associate, four to a large molecule, the

---

* Tyr-His-His-Phe-Phe-Asp-His-Ser-Asp-Ser-His-Phe-Asp-Phe-His-Phe.

41. Calvin, M. (1969) Proc. Roy. Soc. Edinburgh. Series B. 70, 273.
42. Ingram, V. M. (1962) Fed. Proc. 21, 1053.

primary structure of myoglobin must undergo alterations at many sites. On this, John T. Edsall has made the following observations. "Such changes cannot happen all at once; they must occur in many stages, over a long period of time. The intermediate mutational forms, we would suppose, must be rather unsatisfactory proteins, with imperfect tendencies to form loose aggregates of monomers, but without the advantageous cooperative interactions of haemoglobin as we know it. They would be neither good myoglobin nor good haemoglobin, and the organisms that possessed such molecules would scarcely be expected to do well in the ordeal of natural selection."[43] These remarks would apply even if we supposed that myoglobin and haemoglobin derived from an ancestral gene. What would be the function of such a gene product?

DESIGN FOR AN ENZYME

The basic principles and strategy for the chemical synthesis of peptides have been described.[44,45] The classical methods of peptide synthesis have been invaluable and discovery of the solid-phase technique by Merrifield has greatly enhanced the speed and accuracy of peptide synthesis. The specific synthesis of various polypeptidyl hormones, ferredoxin, synthetic antigens, and partial enzyme sequences has been crowned by recent reports of the total synthesis of the enzyme ribonuclease, containing 124 amino acids, which possesses true enzymatic activity toward its natural substrate.[46,47] Lists of naturally occurring peptides and proteins which were synthesised in the years

43. Edsall, J. T. (1968) in *Structural Chemistry and Molecular Biology.* Rich, A. and Davidson, N. (eds.) W. H. Freeman and Co. p. 88.
44. Merrifield, R. B. (1969) *Adv. in Enzymol.* 32, 221.
45. *Chemistry and Biology of Peptides.* Meienhofer, J. (ed.) Ann Arbor Science Publishers Inc., Ann Arbor, Michigan 48106 (1972).
46. Gutte, B. and Merrifield, R. B. (1969) *J. Am. Chem. Soc.* 91, 501.
47. A series of five communications by a group of workers in the *J. Am. Chem. Soc.* 91 (1969) 502-508.

up to 1976 are available.[48]

We have seen that short peptides of predetermined sequence can be synthesised to serve as models of enzymatic catalysis. In this section we will examine some of the thinking and experiments concerning the random synthesis of such peptides, in conditions simulating those of the primitive earth.

Polymerisation Agents

There appears to be no lack of agents, chemical and physical, that aid the polymerisation of amino acids. The effects of heat alone,[49] or heat with various forms of phosphate,[50,51] on mixtures of amino acids produced "proteinoids"—with protein-like characteristics. Anhydrous conditions and the presence of excess dicarboxylic (aspartic, glutamic) or diamino (lysine) acids were essential ingredients. The L-amino acids undergo racemisation during the process[49] and secondary peptide linkages through the non-alpha carboxyl groups of aspartic and glutamic acids may be expected. Polymetaphosphate ethyl ester has also been used as a condensing agent but, due to its ready hydrolysis by water, it requires organic solvents.

Carbodiimides, R.N:C:N.R, in particular, NN—dicyclohexyl-carbodiimide, have proved to be useful reagents for the synthesis of peptides. Cyanamide, dicyanamide, and dicyandiamide are able to tautomerise to reactive carbodiimide forms and thus promote synthesis. These compounds are derived from HCN and can function in an aqueous environment at moderate temperatures. The role

48. *Amino-acids, Peptides, and Proteins.* A Specialist Periodical Report. Sheppard, R. C. (Senior Reporter). The Chemical Society. Burlington House, London WIV OBN, Vols. 5-7 (1974-1976).
49. Fox, S. W. and Harada, K. (1960) *J. Am. Chem. Soc.* 82, 3745.
50. Harada, K. and Fox, S. W. (1965) in *The Origins of Prebiological Systems.* Fox, S. W. (ed.) Academic Press. p. 289.
51. Vegotsky, A. and Fox, S. W. (1959) *Fed. Proc.* 18, 343.

of dicyanamide in dipeptide synthesis has been studied in detail.[52] An undissociated amino acid carboxyl group is required, which means that the pH must be kept low, at about 2.[53] The coupling of certain amino acids having side-chains which absorb light in the 240-280 mu range by dicyanamide is facilitated by UV irradiation.[54]

We may therefore say that different polymerising influences, such as heat and cyanamide derivatives, could have operated on amino acids to produce peptides in the primordial earth. Certain constraints are also apparent; such as the requirement of excess diamino or dicarboxylic acids in the thermal condensation process, and a low pH when cyanamide compounds are involved. The substrate for these reactions would have been D and L amino acids, predominantly glycine and alanine. The products would be complex and very likely branched because of the reactive side-chains of aspartic, glutamic acids, and lysine. In modern synthesis of peptides these side-chains, and those of cysteine and arginine, are meticulously "masked." In abiotic synthesis such peptides as were formed must have been rather bizarre and unbiological. In the laboratory, the pyro-condensation of aspartic acid produces at least 33% of peptide linkages of the β type.[55]

Experimental evidence has been adduced, however, to support the thesis that

a. a mechanism for the formation of α peptides could have functioned[56]

---

52. Steinman, G., Kenyon, D. H., and Calvin, M. (1966) *Biochim. Biophys. Acta,* 124, 339.

53. Steinman, G., Lemmon, R. M., and Calvin, M. (1967) *Science,* 147, 1574.

54. *Biochemical Predestination,* Kenyon, D. H. and Steinman, G. McGraw-Hill Book Co. (1969) p. 191.

55. Kovacs, J., Kovacs, H. N., Konyves, I., Csaszar, J., Vajda, T., and Mix, H. (1961) *J. Org. Chem.* 26, 1084.

56. a. Akabori, S. (1959) in *The Origin of Life on the Earth* Clark, F. and Synge, R. L. M. (eds.) Pergamon Press. p. 189.
    b. Steinman, C. (1966) *Science,* 154, 1344.

b. a degree of non-randomness and even order was present in the primitive polymerisation of amino acids. This has been suggested by the quantitative composition of proteinoids[57] and the comparison of experimentally produced dipeptide yields with frequencies of dipeptide sequences from known protein sequences.[58]

The mechanism suggested for (a) has the following experimental basis. Since the side-chains of glycine and alanine are unreactive in peptide bond formation, polymers of these acids will be the biological α type. The next step calls for the conversion of the side-chains. For instance, under the influence of an electrical discharge, the side-chain of alanine ($-CH_3$) is convertible to the β-carboxyl of aspartic acid.[56] Polyglycine heated (60-100C) in the presence of kaolinate, aqueous formaldehyde, and K_2CO_3, $NaHCO_3$, or triethylamine, produced a polymer which, on hydrolysis, liberated serine.[56a] Threonyl and allothreonyl residues were produced with acetaldehyde in place of formaldehyde. With formaldehyde, 2 - 3% of glycyl residues of polyglycine were converted to seryl residues and, with acetaldehyde, the rate of conversion of glycyl to threonyl residues was about 1.5% These are the rates for polymers containing 140 to 170 glycyl residues. However it is not usually appreciated that proteins undergo a remarkable variety of reactions with formaldehyde.[59] And acetaldehyde causes extensive "browning" of proteins from reaction with primarily the amino groups.

57. Fox, S. W., Harada, K., Woods, K. R., and Windsor, C. R. (1963) Arch. Biochem. Biophys. 102, 439.
58. a. Steinman, G. (1967) Arch. Biochem. Biophys. 121, 533.
    b. Steinman, G. and Cole, M. N. (1967) Proc. Natl. Acad. Sci., 58, 735.
    c. Steinman, G. and Cole, M. N. (1969) Unpublished results quoted in Ref. 54, p. 209.
59. Franekel-Conrat, H. (1951) in Amino Acids and Proteins Greenberg, D. M. (ed.) C. C. Thomas, Springfield, Illinois. p. 532.

NON-RANDOMNESS AND SELECTIVITY

The phenomenon of non-randomness and order in the condensation of amino acids is interesting. In a series of experiments on the thermal copolymerisation of amino acids (170 C for 6 hours) the products were acid-hydrolysed and analysed by ion-exchange chromatography.[49,57] The results of the amino acid analyses were tabulated and compared with those of a "typical natural protein," carbonic anhydrase.[60] Unfortunately it is difficult to select a typical natural protein, as an inspection of the composition of various proteins will show;[61] this being one of the reasons for disparate biuret values.[62] The preponderance of aspartic and glutamic acids in the proteinoids is due to the fact that the anhydrous mixture from which they originate contains 2 parts by weight each of aspartic and glutamic acid and one part of an equimolar assortment of sixteen other acids. Even so it is interesting to note that in some natural proteins (for example, horse heart cytochrome c, calf thymus histones) the glutamic acid fraction tends to be larger than the aspartic acid fraction, whereas the reverse situation obtains in proteinoids.

It was also found that bacterial proteases, chymotrypsin, and pepsin attack the proteinoids, from which it may be inferred that at least some peptide bonds were available to enzyme action.[49] The proteinoids were tested for antigenicity in rabbits and guinea pigs with negative results. As the polymers had mean molecular weights in the range 3000-9000 the factor of molecular size does not fully account for their non-antigenicity. Synthetic polymers of

---

60. Ref. 54, p. 208.
61. Tristram, G. R. and Smith, R. H. (1963) in *The Proteins,* Academic Press, Vol. 1, p. 45.
62. *Molecular Biology of Human Proteins,* Schultze, H. E. and Heremans, J. F. Elsevier Publishing Company. (1966) Vol. 1, p. 173-235.

molecular weights around 10,000 have been shown to be immunogenic.[63] Among these are polymers made up of only three kinds of amino acids (Ala[38], Glu[52], Tyr[10], M.W., 4, 100), and polylysine built on a "backbone" of poly-DL-alanine and tyrosine, of molecular weight 6,000. More likely the proteinoids, composed of D and L amino acids, were not antigenic for the same reasons that polypeptides composed of the "unnatural" D amino acids are usually not antigenic. The reasons for this are discussed by Sela.[63]

Reports that the distribution of peaks obtained by fractionating proteinoid on the DEAE-cellulose column bear comparison with the elution **pattern** of turtle serum proteins adds nothing to the claim that amino acids condense thermally in some sort of an order.[64] [We have already noted that nucleosides with unnatural linkages behave in a. similar way on chromatography as their natural congeners (p. 43)].

We will now examine the type of non-randomness arising from selectivity exercised by the growing point of a peptide chain. In this regard the results of Steinman and Cole[58b] are relevant and, in fact, have been quoted by Calvin[41,65] and by Kenyon and Steinman[54,48c] in support of the plausibility of this mechanism. The procedure was to bind an amino acid by its carboxyl group to a resin and react its free amino end with the carboxyl of a second amino acid. A number of dipeptides was thus prepared from glycine, alanine, leucine, isoleucine, valine, and phenylalanine. The following table shows the results obtained.

---

63. Sela, M. (1966) *Adv. in Immunol.* 5, 29.
64. Fox. S. W. (1971) in *Prebiotic and Biochemical Evolution* Kimball, A. P. and Oro', J. (eds.) North-Holland Publishing Co. Amsterdam-London, p. 8.
65. *Chemical Evolution,* Calvin, M. Clarendon Press. Oxford (1969) p. 169.

TABLE 4[58b]

A comparison of experimentally prepared dipeptide yields with the frequencies calculated from known protein sequences.

	Values [Relative to GLY-GLY]	
Dipeptide	Experimental	Calculated
Gly-Gly	1.0	1.0
Gly-Ala	0.8	0.7
Ala-Gly	0.8	0.6
Ala-Ala	0.7	0.6
Gly-Val	0.5	0.2
Val-Gly	0.5	0.3
Gly-Leu	0.5	0.3
Leu-Gly	0.5	0.2
Gly-Ile	0.3	0.1
Ile-Gly	0.3	0.1
Gly-Phe	0.1	0.1
Phe-Gly	0.1	0.1

The dipeptides are listed in order of increasing volume of the sidechains of the constituent amino acid residues. The second member of the pair was fixed first to the resin.

Gly = glycine   Ala = alanine   Val = valine   Leu = leucine   Ile = isoleucine   Phe = phenylalanine

If we look at the left-hand column of figures there is an ob-vious over-all trend of decreasing yields as the side-chains of the amino acids concerned get bulkier. From physical considerations alone this phenomenon would not be altogether unexpected. Do these sequences have any biological significance, or are they merely interesting biochemical observations? To answer this question the frequencies of appearance of such pairs of amino acids were looked for among sequences of proteins.[66] The pairs were found and related to the frequency of occurrence of glycyl-glycyl in the particular protein. These calculated frequencies appear on the right column in Table 4. What is often forgotten when the figures in the Table are quoted is the fact that certain vital assumptions were made in arriving at the calculated frequencies. In their original paper Steinman and Cole[58b] suggested that the side-chains of certain amino acids in the proteins, whose sequences they used, could have been produced from non-polar members of an original, less variegated polymer chain. Whenever a serine or threonine appeared in a protein sequence, for example, it was counted as glycine; aspartyl and glutamyl residues were counted as alanine. The basis for these assumptions is the work of Akabori[56a] and Steinman.[56b] We have already discussed the doubtful application of these experimental findings to chemical evolution. Steinman and Cole commented on the adoption of these assumptions in these terms. "It is true that such an assignment may not be entirely valid in all cases since plausible means for the prebiotic production of free serine and aspartic acid monomers have been demonstrated and such units could have participated in peptide synthesis. However, for the reasons noted, these corrections were made here since the calculation was meant to be an approximation and only over-all trends were sought."[67]

The value of the assumption of amino acid equivalence in demonstrating even "over-all trends" is on shaky ground. An inspection of some of the protein sequences used by Steinman and Cole—yeast cytochrome c, egg lysozyme, sperm whale myoglobin, bovine chymotrypsinogen A and bovine ribonuclease—is fairly revealing.[15] If

---

66. Eck, R. V. and Dayhoff, M. O. (1966) *Atlas of Protein Structure and Function,* National Biomedical Foundation, Silver Spring, Maryland.

67. Ref. 58b, p. 737.

glycine, alanine, and the amino acids said to be derived from them are culled from these sequences and their number summed they will be found to constitute **almost half** of the total number of amino acids for each protein. The percentages for the proteins listed are, in order, 47, 52, 43, 54, and 54%. In these calculations cysteine is not considered as equivalent to glycine via modification of serine.[56a] If comparisons are made in these circumstances it would be the absence of an approximation or trend that would be more surprising! In spite of this a difference of 29% exists between experimental and calculated values for five comparisons and in two the difference is 30% (Table 4).

In another approach, the fit between an enzyme and its substrate has inspired experiments to test whether, in the presence of model substrates, something resembling an active site sequence could preferentially be created. In one experimental system the yield of α aspartyl-serine was increased in the ratio of 1.4 in the presence of dimethylformamide (0.1M) as compared to the yield in its absence.[58b] Similar results were said to have been obtained with N-methylacetamide, methyl acetate, and ethyl formate as "substrate." These studies are interesting but due allowance should be made for possible solvent effects so that the interpretation may be less equivocal. Even then, current concepts of an "induced" rather than a preformed fit between enzyme and substrate will pose a problem that is not easy to explain.

Thus far we have been dealing with synthesis of dipeptides. The investigators themselves are only too aware of the modulating forces brought into play when growth extends beyond the dipeptide stage. For then interactions between the incoming amino acid and the terminal, as well as the internal, portions of the polymer will determine what amino acid will next be added on the growing chain.

STEREOSPECIFICITY AMONG PROTEINS

Proteins are L amino acids united through α-peptide bonds. A racemic mixture of D and L amino acids is not compatible with the formation of a polymer in the α-configuration. There is therefore considerable enthusiasm to investigate means which can lead to the spontaneous formation of optically active amino acids.[68] The subject of asymmetric synthesis of organic compounds has been reviewed recently.[69]

Suggestions have been made over the years that circularly polarised light may direct the synthesis of optically active compounds; that one optical isomer may spontaneously crystallise from a racemic mixture, or be selectively absorbed on asymmetric crystals; and that L and D monomers of amino acids may exert some stereoselective action during peptide bond formation.[70] Most of these suggestions, and others of a similar kind, have not been confirmed experimentally.[71] In careful experiments with optically active quartz powders and columns the Amariglios were unable to demonstrate asymmetric synthesis.[72] Degens and his coworkers at Woods Hole, Massachusetts, have recently demonstrated that L aspartate tends to polymerise to a greater extent on kaolinite (aluminium silicate) than D aspartate or a DL mixture. 25% of the L-acid had polymerised after 4 weeks compared to 3% of the D-acid. The nature of the polymers formed, as aspartate has 2 carboxyl groups and an amino group, should be interesting. Another noteworthy feature, pointed out by the authors themselves, is the marked degree of racemisation that the remaining free amino acids underwent as indicated by the loss of optical activity in the supernatant.[73]

---

68. Wald, G. (1957) *Ann. N.Y. Acad. Sci.* 60, 352.
69. Bonner, W. A. (1972) in *Exobiology.* Ponnamperuma, C. (ed.) North-Holland Publishing Co. Amsterdam-London, p. 170.
70. Steinman, G. (1967) *Experientia* 23, 177.
71. Ref. 54, p. 216.
72. Amariglio, A. and Amariglio, H. (1971) in *Chemical Evolution and the Origin of Life.* Buvet, R. and Ponnamperuma, C. (eds.) North-Holland Publishing Co. Vol. 1, p. 63.
73. Degens, E. T., Matheja, J., and Jackson, T. (1970) *Nature,* 227, 492.

Calvin[65] has drawn attention to the work of Gillard and Allen[74] and that of Collman and Kimura[75] on some coordination complexes of cobalt. Buckingham and his colleagues had earlier shown that the complex of cobalt and triethylenetetramine, with its two reactive coordination sites, can react with peptides in aqueous solution in such a way that the N-terminal amino acid residue is hydrolytically cleaved off the peptide chain to form a chelate ring with the complex ion.[76] Significantly, the process involves no racemisation of optically active centres of the dipeptides used for the hydrolysis. Allen and Gillard, working with ethylenediamine cobalt complexes, were able to demonstrate that the dipeptide could select either the D or L forms of the cobalt complex in forming the cobalt-ethylenediamine-dipeptide intermediate. A dipeptide with a C-terminal amino acid of the L configuration causes the dipeptide to combine with the cobalt-ethylenediamine complex in the L configuration, regardless of whether the N-terminal amino acid was D or L. This selection was preferential and not absolute. For instance, in the hydrolysis of glycyl-L-phenylalanine 70% of the cobalt complexes which took part in the reaction were of the L configuration, while 30% were of the D configuration. The reaction may be given as:

$$\text{L-cobalt complexes} \rightleftharpoons \text{D-cobalt complexes} \quad (1)$$

$$\text{Gly-L-Phe} + \text{L-cobalt complex} \longrightarrow \underset{\underset{\displaystyle \text{Gly (70\%)}}{\diagdown \diagup}}{\text{L-cobalt complex}} + \text{L-Phe} \quad (2)$$

$$\text{Gly-L-Phe} + \text{D-cobalt complex} \longrightarrow \underset{\underset{\displaystyle \text{Gly (30\%)}}{\diagdown \diagup}}{\text{D-cobalt complex}} + \text{L-Phe} \quad (3)$$

---

74. Allen, D. E. and Gillard, R. D. (1967) *Chem. Comm.* 1091.
75. Collman, J. P. and Kimura, E. (1967) *J. Am. Chem. Soc.* 89, 6096.
76. Buckingham, D. A., Collman, J. P., Harper, D. A. R., and Marsilli, L. C. (1967) *J. A. Chem. Soc.* 89, 1082.

Collman and Kimura made the surprising discovery that certain novel cobalt complexes actually promoted the formation of dipeptide complexes from glycine esters. Similar peptide and glycinamide complexes were prepared from glycylglycine esters or glycinamides. In view of these experimental results Calvin suggested:[41,65]

a. An autocatalytic system for the accumulation of one optical form of a dipeptide. The preservation of glycyl-D-phenylalanine may be taken as an example, if reaction rates favoured the destruction of glycyl-L-phenylalanine. Since the D and L forms of the starting cobalt complexes are in equilibrium, whichever series begins the reaction pulls the equilibrium to its own favour.

Two factors militate against such a scheme operating. Firstly, the N-terminal amino acid residue resulting from hydrolysis becomes irreversibly coordinated to the metal and secondly, the reaction is, in fact, stoichiometric. The autocatalysis, suggested by Calvin, occurs only when the amino acid as a ligand is capable of being displaced by a second dipeptide. This has not been shown to be possible. Since the reactions were stoichiometric the equilibrium between the D and L forms of the starting cobalt complexes would not be appreciably altered. The stereoselectivity of the mechanism would be drastically hampered.

b. A replicating polypeptide system which does not involve nucleic acid. This mechanism supposes that when the growing polypeptide chain has incorporated some specific amino acids, this signals the attachment of cobalt to the growing end. The bound cobalt is capable of swinging to the front end of the chain to clip off a dipeptide. The latter replicates the original chain, though how it can accomplish this with any precision is not stated.

The more serious objection to this hypothesis is its discord with the experimental findings from which it sprang. No dipeptide complex was ever formed as a cleavage product with either glycylglycylglycine or tetraglycine,[76] although under drastic conditions glycylglycine coordinated as a tridentate ligand. The method was significant because it selectively modified peptide chains be removing a single N-terminal residue under mild conditions. Collman and Kimura were of the opinion that their method would probably not be useful in peptide synthesis. "Once a peptide bond is formed on the metal (cobalt), it would be difficult to remove the peptide without hydrolysis. Furthermore, the labilisation of hydrogens in the chelate ring makes the racemisation of asymmetric centres probable."[75]

CONCLUSION

In conclusion, we can say that while a prima facie case may be made, from some experimental findings, for the role of metal coordination complexes in the chemical evolution of either D or L peptides, the exact nature of this role is unknown. The comment of Steinman in the report of his work on stereoselectivity in peptide synthesis is a fair summary of our present knowledge—"the synthesis of stereohomogenous polypeptide would have had to depend on chance associations at the simple peptide level and then on stabilisation of homopolymers by the α-helix at higher degrees of polymerisation."[70] Bonner (1972)[69] conluded his extensive review of molecular chirality by agreeing with Briggs that, "the origins of optical activity present problems to the hypothesis of chemical evolution that are at present insoluble."

We have reviewed man's many ingenious attempts to synthesise enzymes on the basis of prebiotic conditions. The results of these experiments have not been rewarding enough. Yet around us and within us these little bundles of folded protein perform their catalytic wonders ceaselessly, each as if designed for its task.

Hall and Knowles studied the rates of enolisation of dihydroxyacetone phosphate and of glyceraldehyde 3-phosphate in neutral solution—uncatalysed and catalysed by triose phosphate isomerase. "It is evident that the enzyme has reached the end of its evolutionary development . . . . Further lowering of the free energy barriers for the covalency changes, or destabilisation of any of the enzyme-bond intermediates would have no effect on the flux of substrate, or, therefore, on the effect of the isomerase as a catalyst."[77]

What a magnificent tribute to the forces of mutation and natural selection!

77. Hall, A. and Knowles, J. R. (1975) *Biochemistry* 14, 4348.

Chapter 5

The Evolution of
Proteins

INTRODUCTION

The sequences of amino acids in proteins are being explored as a basis for classifying life-forms and for showing the degree of their relatedness to each other.[1-6] This has been made possible by the availability of sequences for a fairly large number of proteins backed by the analytical prowess of modern high-speed computers to store and collate data. Among the more recently published amino acid sequences are those on pig heart muscle aspartate amino-transferase,[7] Staphylococcus aureus penicillinase,[8] chick skin collagen,[9] dogfish trypsin.[10] It is a tacit assumption that the very fact that we can study the evolution of proteins supports the reality of Neo-Darwinian evolution by mutation and natural selection. This in turn gives the investigation of the origin of life a much-needed psychological fillip. For if proteins of organisms living today could be traced back to their ancestral forms, then there is still hope that these ancestral forms were part of and functioning in the elusive primordial cells which laboratories have

1. *Molecules and Evolution.* Jukes, T. H. Columbia University Press. New York and London (1966).
2. *Biochemical Evolution and the Origin of Life.* Schoffeniels, E. (ed.) North-Holland Publishing Co. Amsterdam-London. Vol. 2 (1971).
3. *Prebiotic and Biochemical Evolution.* Kimball, A. P. and Oro', J. (eds.) North-Holland Publishing Co. Amsterdam-London. (1971).
4. *Atlas of Protein Sequence and Structure.* Dayhoff, M. O. Washington D.C.: National Biomedical Research Foundation. Vol. 5 (1972).
5. *Handbook of Protein Sequences.* Croft, L. R. Joynson-Bruvvers Ltd. Oxford (1973).
6. Florkin, M. (1975) in *Comprehensive Biochemistry.* Florkin, M. and Stotz, E. H. (eds.) Elsevier. Scientific Publishing Co. Vol. 29, Part B.
7. This and the sequences of three other proteins are reported in *Biochem. J.* (1975) 149: 271, 497, 675.
8. Ambler, R. P. (1975) *Biochem. J.* 151, 197.
9. Highberger, J. H., Corbett, C., Kang, A. H., and Gross, J. (1975) *Biochemistry,* 14, 2872. The structures of cardiotoxin from two species of cobra are reported on p. 2860, 2865.
10. Titani, K., Ericsson, L. H., Neurath, H., and Walsh, K. A. (1975) *Biochemistry,* 14, 1358.

been trying to produce. Already opinions have been expressed, and not without basis, that the laboratory approach of imitating a once-for-all event of making a living cell is proving fruitless. Thorpe, characteristically outspoken, recently said, "I think it is fair to say that all the facile speculations and discussion published during the last 10-15 years explaining the mode of the origin of life have been shown to be far too simple-minded and to bear very little weight. The problem in fact seems as far from solution as it ever was."[11]

Sufficient time has elapsed to allow an assessment of the study of proteins in relation to evolution. J. Williams recently reviewed the subject[12] and Ambler and Wynn have discussed at some length the precautions that need to be taken to ensure accuracy and reliability in sequence determination.[13] The working hypothesis is that proteins have undergone point mutations resulting, generally, in one amino acid being exchanged for another. Some of these mutations were accepted because they conferred an advantage or at least did not alter the function of the protein in a lethal way. Families of proteins were thus built up over millions of years which are related to each other and to their ancestral proteins. So we have today a family among the insulins, myoglobins, growth hormones, and so on. When the linear positions of amino acids in two proteins of the same family match they are judged to be homologous, that is, they have a common ancestry. Homology is also considered as present where amino acids are not identical but chemically similar. For instance, a valine is equivalent to a leucine residue in that both have hydrophobic side chains. Considerations of

11. Thorpe, W. H. in *Studies in the Philosophy of Biology*. Ayala, F. J. and Dobzhansky, T. (eds.) Macmillan (1974), p. 116.
12. Williams, J. (1974) in *Chemistry of Macromolecules*. *Biochemistry Series One*. Vol. 1, Gutfreund, H. (ed.) MTP International Review of Science. Butterworth. University Park Press. p. 1.
13. Ambler, R. P. and Wynn, M. (1974) *Biochem. J.* 131, 485.

homology are subjected to statistical analysis to demonstrate whether any similarities are significantly more than would be expected by chance in comparing random arrangements of the same set of amino acids. Furthermore some families are apparently more amenable to the construction of phylogenetic trees than others. Proteins which have changed very little appear of limited value. The histones are an example. In 1.5 billion years they have only accumulated 2 changes among their 102 residues; at the beginning of which period, it is said, the histone lines leading to pea and cattle began to diverge. Haemoglobin mutates rapidly—about 12 accepted point mutations per 100 million years—and fibrinopeptides even more. For our purpose protein families would be too recent in evolutionary time to enable any information on life's earliest beginnings to be gleaned.

CYTOCHROME C

The single polypeptide chain of cytochrome c has been studied in considerable detail. This protein is found in the mitochondria of all living things above the level of bacteria and blue-green algae. The primary structures of more than 30 species are known. In mammals the molecule contains 104 residues with an N-acetylated N terminal group. In insects the number is 108, in mushrooms 108 to 110, and in plants 112. It has been known for some time already that the amino acid residues in 35 positions are unchanged in all cytochromes c studied. X-ray diffraction studies of the three-dimensional structure have made abundantly clear why certain sequences are so well conserved.[14] With horse heart and tuna cytochromes c (M.W. 13,000) as models, the following features are notable.

1. The haem group is housed in a cage lined by amino acids with hydrophobic side chains.

---

14. Muirhead, H. (1974) Ref. 12, p. 57.

2. The 5th and 6th octahedral valencies of the iron atom of haem are filled by coordination with His 18 and Met 80.
3. Two "channels" filled with hydrophobic side chains lead from the haem cage to the surface of the molecule.
4. The 19 lysyl residues are distributed around the entrances of the two channels creating 2 positively charged areas. These are thought to be essential in binding with cytochrome oxidase. A negatively charged patch is located between and away from the two positive patches. This patch is thought to bind to membrane phospholipids.
5. Both the haem group and certain amino acids shift their positions as the oxidation state changes.

We see that there are tight constraints on the molecule that require it to interact in a coordinated manner with its two enzymes (cytochrome oxidase and reductase) as well as with membrane. Small wonder therefore that tremendous selection pressures are postulated to act in preserving the conformation of the molecule. There are many point mutations which are forbidden by natural selection. Precisely here we should also wonder at the antiquity of this remarkable protein. How did a non-protein haem group come to fit nicely into a hydrophobic protein pocket with just the right ancillary channels for electron transport? The stringent conservation of parts of the primary sequence spread **over the molecule** carries the inescapable conclusion that the first cytochrome c must have had these same sequences intact, or it would have suffered elimination by natural selection as being unfit. Since it has survived, it has apparently done so by arresting changes to the vital sequences. The first cytochrome c must have been functional de novo. This calls to mind the remarks of Ponnamperuma and Sweeney on the origin of life. "But for an extraordinary event such as the origin of life, an extraordinary, catastrophic single cause can be considered. After all, it is not necessary that such an event be repeated continually. Life had only to arise once." It looks as if cytochrome c, like so many other biologically important molecules, had only to arise once.

THE ART OF MATCHING SEQUENCES TO SHOW HOMOLOGY

Let us return to consider other aspects of proteins and evolution. In trying to show degrees of relatedness among members of a family it is common practice to insert gaps at awkward places. This device has the merit of bringing the rest of the molecule into better alignment. An example from Williams follows.[15] In comparing the cytochromes c of the fruit fly and the horse it is advantageous to disregard the first four residues of the insect sequence and the C-terminal acid of the horse sequence. By so doing between 70 to 80% of the amino acids match.

FRUIT FLY:GLY-VAL-PRO-ALA-GLY-ASP-VAL......ALA-THR-LYS
   HORSE: Acetyl-GLY-ASP-VAL......ALA-THR-ASN-GLU

Another example of family resemblance is that between the pancreatic proteases trypsinogen and chymotrypsinogen.[16] The introduction of a small number of gaps led to large increases in the number of matches. This measure fails with pancreatic ribonuclease and lysozyme, two functionally different enzymes.[17] Utilising their computer technique, which corrects for altered limits of random expectations when inserting gaps, Haber and Koshland evaluated the relatedness among certain human γ-globulins. Not unexpectedly the sequences were found to be related to each other beyond the expectations of chance. The pleasant surprise is that "the computer simulations indicate that there is little justification for considering the sequences with gaps to be a more accurate alignment than the sequences without gaps." Homology is best demonstrated with proteins which, on other grounds, are

---

15. Ref. 12, p. 13.
16. Walsh, K. A. and Neurath, H. (1964) *Proc. Nat. Acad. Sci.*, Wash. 52, 884.
17. Haber, J. E. and Koshland, D. E. (1970) *J. Mol. Biol.* 50, 617.

expected to be homologous! One suspects, on the same line of reasoning, that the homology said to exist between bovine α-lactalbumin and hen egg lysozyme is forced. With 6 gaps in the former and 2 in the latter 45 identical matches for 123 residues could be discerned and a further 23 positions concurred, only if one accepted the assumption that chemically similar amino acids should be regarded as matching. One then comes up with the observation that these two proteins possess greater homology (relatedness) than do whale myoglobin and horse haemoglobin! Why bovine α-lactalbumin should be homologous with hen egg lysozyme requires explanation. Attempts to press a homology between cytochrome c_{551} of Pseudomonas and the larger cytochrome c of higher organisms have foundered on the extensive gaps that are clearly needed to align the sequences.[18] Ambler and Wynn carefully sequenced cytochromes c_{551} from three closely related species of Pseudomonas.[19] They showed that the differences between pairs of sequences range from 22-39%. The difference of cytochrome sequences between mammals and insects is 33% and that between mammals and amphibians is 18%! The authors commented, ''The large differences observed between proteins from relatively closely related bacteria suggest that differences in corresponding proteins from more diverse microorganisms may be so great that indications of a common evolutionary origin will not be obvious.''

PHYLOGENETIC TREES FROM PROTEIN SEQUENCES

Nevertheless it has become customary to draw phylogenetic trees from comparisons of the amino acid se-

18. Dickerson, R. E. (1971) *J. Mol. Biol.* 57, 1.
19. Ambler, R. P. and Wynn, M. (1973) *Biochem. J.* 131, 485.

quences of families of proteins.[4,21] Perhaps the best known is that for cytochrome c (Fig. 16).

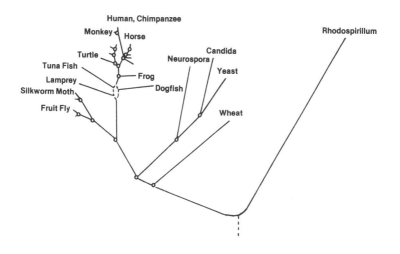

Figure 16. Abbreviated phylogenetic tree of cytochrome c based on Ref. 20.

The Time Factor

Jukes and Holmquist observed that the **magnitude** of amino acid differences among certain vertebrates as well as their relationship to **time** should be taken into account if anomalies are not to crop up. "Such anomalies show up on 'phylogenetic trees' as apparently negative rates of evolutionary divergence, or incorrect taxonomic placement of an organism in the wrong family."[22] In an earlier study Fitch and Margoliash found that the molecular

20. Dayhoff, M. O. and Park, C. M. (1969) in *Atlas of Protein Sequence and Structure.* Dayhoff, M. O. (ed.). National Biomedical Research Foundation. Vol. 4, p. 9.
21. Goodman, M., Barnabas, J., Matsuda, G., and Moore, G. W. (1971) *Nature,* 233, 604
22. Jukes, T. H. and Holmquist, R. (1972). *Science,* 177, 532.

phylogenetic tree produced disparities with classical zoological schemes. The turtle appeared more closely related to the bird than to its fellow reptile the rattlesnake.[23] Jukes and Holmquist explained that such a disparity stems from the two reptiles having diverged rapidly during evolution. They suggest that the evolutionary rate of change of cytochromes c is species-dependent as well as time-dependent.

Differences between	Number of different amino acid residues per 100 codons
Rattlesnake/turtle	21
Chicken/lamprey	17
Horse/dogfish	16
Dog/screw-worm fly	15

The difference between turtle and rattlesnake is notably larger than differences found between widely separated zoological classes or even two different phyla. On fibrinopeptide sequences the kangaroo, a marsupial, is grouped with the carnivore branch, in contrast to conventional mammalian phylogeny.[21]

There is an unwarranted assumption of uniform mutation rates and selective pressures in drawing up phylogenetic trees, a fact highlighted by Krzywicki and Slonimski.[24] Let us say that we have three related proteins such that **A** and **B** are similar and both differ from **C**. A phylogenetic tree can be drawn to emphasise the relationship of (**A**,**B**)

23. Fitch, W. M. and Margoliash, E. (1967) 155, 279.
24. Krzywicki, A. and Slonimski, P. O. (1968). *J. Theoret. Biol.* 21, 305.

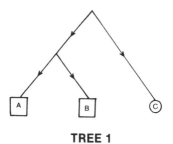

TREE 1

Now if mutation rates and/or selective pressures act more strongly on **C** than on (**A**,**B**) the dissimilarity of **C** from (**A**,**B**) can result from either of the following alternative schemes of evolution.

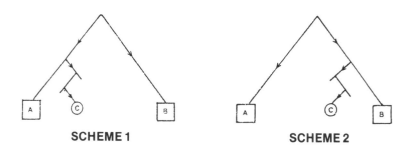

SCHEME 1   **SCHEME 2**

If this were true the correct phylogenetic tree is not TREE 1, but either TREE 2 or 3.

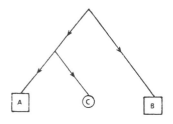

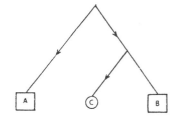

TREE 2
(Result of SCHEME 1)

TREE 3
(Result of SCHEME 2)

The conventional zoological phylogenetic trees have to come in to assist the interpretation of molecular data on this score. Let us return to our earlier example of the rattlesnake and the turtle cytochromes. Confronted with an amino acid difference between the two that **exceeds that between members of different classes** how, otherwise, could Juke and Holmquist have concluded:

a. that the rattlesnake and turtle should **still be in the same class [Reptilia]**, and that, therefore explains away
b. the large difference as having been due to a faster rate of change of cytochrome c, mainly in rattlesnake?

Fitch and Langley argue that, based on certain assumptions, the rates of nucleotide substitutions were not constant during the evolution of several mammalian proteins.[25-27] One conclusion is that the "molecular clock" is more accurate when the proteins used to calibrate it are large in number or taken over a long period of time. Accuracy here means correspondence to paleontological datings, themselves of uncertain accuracy. Another conclusion is that the majority of substitutions are not, after all, neutral. If they were they would be taking place at a uniform rate equal to the neutral mutation rate. As a follow-through it could be further surmised that if amino acid mutations are not neutral they must be reflected in changes in the function of proteins. Such differences, previously not detected, have now been discovered for cytochromes c from a few species. These exhibit individual high affinities for cytochrome c oxidase at low ionic strengths.[28] The extension of these findings is awaited with interest.

---

25. Langley, C. H. and Fitch, W. M. in *Genetic Structure of Populations*. Morton, N. E. (ed.). Honolulu: University of Hawaii Press. (1973). p. 246-262.
26. Langley, C. H. and Fitch, W. M. (1974). *J. Mol. Evol.* 3, 161.
27. Fitch, W. M. and Langley, C. H. (1976). *Federation Proc.* 35, 2092.
28. Ferguson-Miller, S., Brautigan, D. L., and Margoliash, E. (1976). *J. Biol. Chem.* 251, 1104.

The Multiple Change Factor

Where there are two related amino acid sequences, say, ABC and ABD, it is not possible to trace whether ABD came from ABC by (a) a single change, (b) multiple changes, (c) whether both have a common ancestor, or (d) have no ancestral relationship.

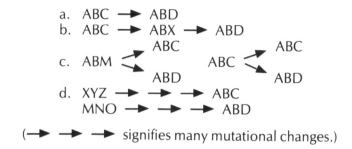

(→ → → signifies many mutational changes.)

Attempts have been made to take into account the probability that such multiple changes have indeed occurred. But Williams doubts the validity of the use of probability theory to correct for multiple changes. The attempts are based on "the unacceptable assumption that amino acid changes occur randomly with equal probabilities at all sites."[29]

THE USE OF MINIMUM MUTATION DISTANCES TO SHOW HOMOLOGY

Each amino acid is coded by three nucleotides. A change in one member of the coding triplet can result in a different amino acid being inserted into a polypeptide chain. More often than not random mutations result in no change or a substitution of an amino acid by one chemically like it. This is due to the fact that the genetic code is degenerate, that is, an amino acid is coded for by

---

29. Ref. 12, p. 37.

more than one nucleotide triplet. So much so that for phenylalanine, valine, isoleucine, or methionine any change in the first or third nucleotide in the respective triplet yields another hydrophobic residue. Presumably in most cases the protein in which such "conservative" changes occur will not have its function impaired. A change in the first base of the triplet codon usually converts one amino acid to another of similar chemical and structural properties. Such an exchange is called "conservative." One must keep in mind that the 20 or so amino acids do have distinct advantages in their own right or they would not have found their niche in the evolutionary process. When we speak of "exchangeable amino acids of equivalent properties" we are using ambivalent terms which need to be qualified by the site of the exchanges. One has only to remember the invariant sequences of cytochrome c to prove the point. Here **no** exchange of any sort is allowed, including equivalent exchanges, so-called. The proposal that a decreased frequency of exchange of a particular amino acid qualifies the exchange being labelled "conservative" is, as Dickerson points out, begging the question. Now the second base is important as it specifies the main chemical nature of the amino acid and changes in this position cause radical substitutions, for example, the conversion of isoleucine (AUA) to arginine (AGA). Jukes (1963)[30] introduced and Fitch (1966)[31] developed the idea that evolutionary relationships can be extracted from DNA sequences as well as amino acid sequences. Should an ancestral protein develop into 2 proteins (evolutionary divergence)—so that the number of identical amino acid residues decreases—one could still work out the number of mutations required to interconvert the two polypeptide sequences. The actual DNA base sequence corresponding to a polypeptide chain is unknown because of the

30. Jukes, T. H. (1963) *Adv. Biol. Med. Phys.* 9, 1.
31. Fitch, W. M. (1966) *J. Mol. Biol.* 16, 1.

degeneracy of the code. The strategy is to choose the optimum pair of triplet codons for each pair of amino acids so that the **minimum number of mutations** is required to interconvert them. Statistical help is needed here to see that the minimum number of mutations is indeed significantly less than that expected of random sequences. Fitch calculated that the average minimum number of base changes per codon was 1.58 for random sequences. It will be less than 1.58 if two related sequences are being compared.

Dickerson draws our attention to a dilemma in interpretation.[18] Let us suppose that an analysis of two polypeptide chains yields a small minimum mutation distance. Does this support the fact that the two chains are related by a common ancestor (homology)? Or does this reflect the phenomenon called convergence—two proteins from two different ancestral forms evolving toward a common chemical structure. As Dickerson neatly sums up: "This procedure confuses divergence from common ancestry with convergence on common function." In fact certain phylogenetic patterns for the hominoids, according to their myoglobins, make it necessary to accept a back mutation or a parallel mutation, a quandary which is not easy to resolve.[32]

Haber and Koshland[17] illustrated the potential error inherent in the minimum mutation distance method using two hypothetical peptide segments:

Asp-Pro-Arg-Ser-His-Glu-Lys
Val-Leu-Leu-Leu-Leu-Val-Met

It will be seen, with the aid of a genetic code table, how a single mutation at each amino acid site can convert one chain into the other. One set of possible mutations is as follows:

GAU-CCG-CGU-UCA-CAC-GAA-AAG
GUU-CUG-CUU-UUA-CUC-GUA-AUG

---

32. Romero-Herrera, A. E., Lehmann, H., and Castillo, O. (1976) *Nature,* 261, 162.

The average mutation value is 1 compared to a random value of 1.58 and yet the two proteins may be totally unrelated. It would seem that in comparing **the genes** (essentially degenerate) rather than **the gene products** no special advantage is gained and a measure of uncertainty is introduced. An analogy may not be out of place. It is as if one, wishing to ascertain if two people share the same profession, has given up comparing their clothes in favour of comparing their tailors.

THE USE OF STRUCTURE TO SHOW HOMOLOGY

In his paper on sequence and structure homologies in bacterial and mammalian-type cytochromes Dickerson asked: "Is tertiary folding a surer guide to ancestral kinship and homology than sequence? Can the same folded structure be retained after two sequences have changed beyond recognition?"

Haemoglobins and myoglobins are good illustrative proteins as their amino acid sequences are known and work with X-ray diffraction techniques has yielded exquisite details on their 3-D structures. The amino acid sequences for the α and β chains of HbA, the γ chain of HbF, and the δ chain of HbA_2 have long been established. On the basis of their amino acid differences Ingram[33] suggested that the α chain might possibly be the oldest among the three chains and might be homologous with the chain of lamprey oxyhaemoglobin. A gene duplication is said to have separated the ancestor of myoglobin genes from that of haemoglobin genes. The succession proposed by Ingram:

α chain $\longrightarrow$ γ chain $\longrightarrow$ β chain $\longrightarrow$ δ chain

is now thought to be,

α chain $\longrightarrow$ β chain $\longrightarrow$ γ chain $\longrightarrow$ δ chain.[21]

The mammalian α genes are deemed to have diverged

---

33. Ingram, V. M. (1961). *Nature*, 189, 704.

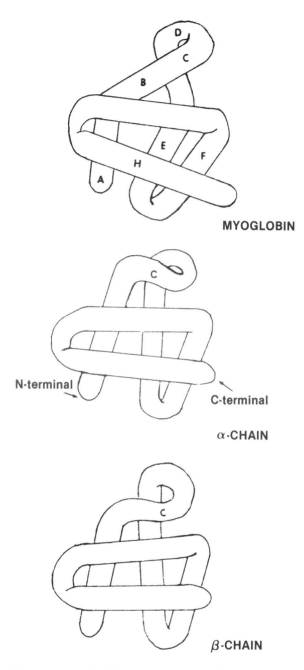

MYOGLOBIN

α·CHAIN

N-terminal

C-terminal

β·CHAIN

Figure 17. Comparison of the folding of myoglobin and the α and β chains of haemoglobin. Note the deletion of the D helix in the α-chain.

the least from the common vertebrate globin ancestor and the myoglobin genes. Human myoglobin agrees with the human α chain in only 16% of identical matches and yet their conformations are similar.

An analysis of the amino acid identities of the E and H helices of human α, β, and γ chains of human haemoglobin is given in Table 5.

TABLE 5

	αE	βE	γE	αH	βH	γH
αE	21	10	10	2	7	3
βE	10	21	14	7	8	5
γE	10	14	21	6	7	6
αH	2	7	6	21	8	10
βH	7	8	7	8	21	13
γH	3	5	6	10	13	21

Numbers indicate amino acid identities. Table modified from Table 4, Ref. 18.

From the relationship grid it is evident that E and H helices of β and γ chains resemble each other. This is difficult to explain as the E helix lines the haem pocket on the molecule's exterior while the H helix is buried in the interior. Yet the E and H helices of the α chain bear little similarity by comparison. As Dickerson observed, "It is hard to see why the same selective forces would not have been at work on the α chains . . . . And why should the H chain of α look more like the E chains of β and γ than its own E chain?"

Apparently undaunted by the previous considerations,

several groups of workers have sought amino acid homologies in structurally related enzyme topologies. Similarities in the NAD-binding domains of the dehydrogenases have lately received such attention accompanied by phylogenetic speculation.[34,35] Of the latter Blake writes, "The prospect of distinguishing theoretically between the rival hypotheses of convergent or divergent evolution on the basis of tertiary structure seems rather remote because it depends on the solution of a number of basic problems of enzyme structure stability that are, as yet, far from being solved."[36]

CONCLUSION

Many serious shortcomings confront the student of protein evolution. We see, for instance, that the assumption of uniform mutation rates among proteins is generally invalid. Nevertheless the establishment of homology—by showing that sequences are related to each other beyond the expectation of chance—forms a worthwhile venture in its own right. Such studies can be pursued quite apart from aspirations to draw up all-embracing phylogenies which, when it comes to validation, have to lean upon palaeontology for support. Boulter and his colleagues have constructed a phylogeny for 15 angiosperm species based upon cytochrome c sequences and have shown that it gives results within taxa which are consistent with morphological classifications. They noted that new phylogenetic insights as a result of their work were limited, and that they did not consider "phylogenetic speculation" to be profitable without data from more se-

34. Ohlsson, I., Nordstrom, B., and Branden, C. I. (1974). *J. Mol. Biol.* 89, 339.
35. Rossmann, M. G., Moras, D., and Olsen, K. W. (1974). *Nature,* 250, 194.
36. Blake, C. C. F. (1975) in *Essays in Biochemistry,* Campbell, P. N. and Aldridge, W. N. (eds.) The Biochemical Society. Academic Press. Vol. 11, pp. 37-79.

quences being available.[37]

Krzywicki and Slonimski summed it up well when they advocated a "second approach" to the study of homologous proteins. "We can leave aside the question how proteins evolved (diachronic approach). Instead we ask what is common in the structure of functionally homologous proteins we find nowadays, i.e. **we can focus our attention on the structure [synchronic approach] disregarding the genesis.**"[38]

Thus α-foetoprotein and albumin share many chemical similarities. Their serum concentrations are high and inversely related. α-foetoprotein could very well be a foetal counterpart of albumin, as sequence homology on 59 residues reveals.[39]

37. Boulter, D., Ranshaw, J. A. M., Thompson, E. W., Richardson, M., and Brown, R. H. (1972). *Proc. R. Soc. Lond. B.* 181, 441.
38. Ref. 24, p. 306.
39. Ruoslahti, E. and Terry, W. D. (1976). *Nature,* 260, 804.

Chapter 6

The Living Cell

"The production of organic molecules for the origin of life is not at all the same as the origin of life."

Carl Sagan[1]

WHAT IS "LIVING"?

The simplest unit of any living organism is the cell. It has not been necessary, so far, to define what "life" means, or to define the structure of the cell because we were concerned with the origin of the specific building blocks of life. What is "life," then? As Pattee pointed out, since most cellular reactions can be demonstrated in vitro the implication is that life is just a collection of DNA, RNA, enzymes, and other molecules in proper spatial relationship. Molecular biology has evaded the central question of what distinguishes life from non-life, and this has satisfied many biologists.[2] The attitude that life can be wholly explained in terms of physical principles and chemistry has been adopted by several writers.[3,4,5] An extreme example of a reductionist view may be the "improved definition of life" given by Professor Bernal as "a partial, continuous, progressive, multiform, and conditionally inter-active self realisation of the potentialities of atomic electron states."[6] Others, notably some physicists, who are unable to explain to their own satisfaction the apparent contravention of the second law of thermodynamics by living things, believe that either some principle is missing from physics,

1. Sagan, C. (1972) in *Exobiology*. Ponnamperuma, C. (ed.) North-Holland Publishing Co., Amsterdam-London, p. 471.
2. Pattee, H. H. (1969) in *Towards a Theoretical Biology*. Waddington, C. H. (ed.) Edinburgh University Press. p. 268.
3. *The Molecular Biology of the Gene*. Watson, J. D. W. A. Benjamin. New York. (1976) 3rd Edition.
4. *Of Molecules and Men*. Crick, F. University of Washington Press. (1966).
5. *Chromosomes, Giant Molecules, and Evolution*. Wallace, B. Macmillan. (1967).
6. *The Origin of Life*. Bernal, J. D. Weidenfeld and Nicolson. (1967). p. 168.

or that life is irreducible to its laws.[7,8,9] There is in living things, at all levels and in almost all their manifestations, an "urge" or "directiveness," a perseverance to maintain their own being.[10] "The claims made following the discovery of DNA, to the effect that all study could be reduced eventually to molecular biology, have shown once more, that the Laplacean ideal of universal knowledge is still the theoretical ideal of the natural sciences . . . . But now the analysis of the hierarchy to ultimate particulars is to wipe out our very sight of it."[7] Or, in the words of Dobzhansky, more recently, "Reductionism is now the semi-official creed of biological establishment. In the form widespread among biologists, it admits only the molecular phenomenae as 'fundamental' really worthy of serious study. No competent biologist known to me denies the interest and importance of molecular biology; the point is simply that it is unwise to close one's eyes to the existence of organismic phenomena, that is, of the phenomena of the levels of integration above the molecular."[11]

Others prefer a third approach, believing that the potential for hereditary evolution is the primary characteristic of life which distinguishes it from other collections of matter. An attempt is made to formulate a satisfactory account of living processes in the language of quantum mechanics and automata theory. "This must include not only an account of how molecular codes and descriptions can originate, but also how they can continue to operate so reliably in a disorderly environment. To the physicist this

7. Polanyi, M. (1968). *Science,* 160, 1308.
8. *Atom and Organism.* Elsasser, W. M. Princeton University Press. (1966).
9. *Science, Man, and Morals.* Thorpe, W. H. Methuen, London. (1965).
10. Mora, P. T. (1963) *Nature,* 199, 212.
11. Dobzhansky, T. (1969) in *The Uniqueness of Man.* Poslansky, J. D. (ed.) North-Holland Publishing Co. p. 43.

still appears as a deep enigma."[12]

In a sense, therefore, when the biologist is confronted with the problem of the nature of life, as in a cell, he becomes some sort of a "neo-vitalist." In a way not yet understood the living organism is more than the sum of its parts. In an operational sense living cells are living because they can perform and integrate a repertoire of functions. Among these are the biosynthesis of self-molecule, the storage and transformation of energy, differentiation and reproduction (through meiosis and mitosis single cells reproduce entire multicellular organisms), and adaptive reactions to stress from the environment.

CELLULAR STRUCTURE AND ORGANISATION

Excellent texts and reviews are available on the cell, its membranes and organelles.[13-17] We will no more than briefly outline cellular structure and indicate those areas which have come up for discussion in the context of the development of morphological complexity.

The simplest cell today is the prokaryote. It is small, having only the cell wall and membrane and no intracellular membranous organelles such as mitochondria, Golgi apparatus, or endoplasmic reticulum. The ribosomes lie free

---

12. Ref. 2, p. 282.
13. *Methods in Membrane Biology.* Korn, E. D. (ed.) Plenum Press. New York and London. (1974) Vols. 1, 2.
14. *Cells and Organelles.* Novkioff, A. B. and Holtzman, E. Holt Rinehart and Winston, Inc. (1970).
15. *The Functioning Cytoplasm.* Bulger, R. E. and Strum, J. M. Plenum Press. New York and London. (1974).
16. *The Mitochondria of Microorganisms.* Lloyd, D. Academic Press, London. New York. San Francisco. (1974).
17. *Biological Transport.* Christensen, H. N. W. A. Benjamin, Inc. Reading, Massachusetts. 2nd ed. (1975).

in the cytoplasm. In place of a nucleus with a definite membrane is found a nuclear zone containing a double-helical DNA strand. The pleuropneumonia-like organisms, spirochaetes, rickettsiae, eubacteria, and blue-green algae are prokaryotes. Of the last about 2000 species are known. These algae are thought to be the most primitive, oxygen-producing plants. In addition to chlorophyll, other unique pigments are present.

Eukaryotic cells are usually thought to be derived from prokaryotes. There are others who believe the reverse to be the case, with good reasons.[18] In any case eukaryotes are larger and far more complex. Their intracytoplasmic organelles include mitochondria, Golgi complex, lysosomes, endoplasmic reticulum, peroxisomes, and a nucleus with a distinct nucleolus, surrounded by a perinuclear envelope with large pores. The DNA is found in several to many chromosomes. Depending on the type of cell, microtubules, cilia, and flagella may also be present. Fungi, protozoa, most algae, and both plant and animal cells are eukaryotic. Organelles, whether simple or complex, possess distinct morphology and function. Interest in them has mounted in recent years because of their possible contributory role to the formation of the pristine cell. Bernal has suggested that the formation of an endothelial reticulum brought a certain number of organelles together and enabled them to function as a complete cell.[19] Sagan has hypothesised that three fundamental organelles, the mitochondria, the photosynthetic plastids and certain basal bodies of flagella were themselves once free-living, prokaryotic cells.[20] The literature on this topic is extensive and we can only men-

18. Reanney, D. C. (1974). *J. Theoret. Biol.* 48, 243.
19. Ref. 6, p. 87.
20. Sagan. L. (1967). *J. Theoret. Biol.,* 14, 225.

tion some recent reviews.[21-24] In the case of the mitochondrion several pieces of evidence seem to militate against the endosymbiosis concept. Roodyn and Wilkie have pointed out that the DNA in the mitochondrion appears to have a very limited coding capacity, possibly only enough for thirty proteins, which is less than the amount required for the total synthesis of a mitochondrion.[21] Fairly substantial criticisms have been levelled against the endosymbiont hypothesis by Lloyd.[25] Furthermore, it is doubtful whether mitochondrial lipids are synthesised in situ. It also appears that mitochondria do not synthesise soluble proteins, such as cytochrome c. Lastly, experiments with yeast show that the anaerobic cell is apparently devoid of discrete mitochondria, which only appear on admission of oxygen. This is not de novo synthesis, however, as electron micrographs of frozen-etched anaerobic yeast cells have clearly revealed the presence of mitochondrial structures which are morphologically quite similar to those observed in aerobically grown yeast cells.[26] Fridovich has conjectured on the bearing that superoxide dismutase has on the origin of mitochondria. He reasons that when confronted with oxygen in the environment both prokaryote and protoeukaryote came up with the same defence—a superoxide dismutase. However these enzymes developed as "separate proteins;" the prokaryotic enzyme had manganese or iron and the protoeukaryotic had copper or zinc. Then a sup-

21. *The Biogenesis of Mitochondria,* Roodyn, D. B. and Wilkie, D. Methuen, London. (1968).
22. Carr, N. G. and Craig, I. W. (1970). in *Phytochemical Phylogeny.* Harborne, J. E. (ed.) Academic Press, p. 119.
23. *Origin and Continuity of Cell Organelles.* Reinert, J. and Ursprung, H. (eds.). Springer-Verlag. Berlin. (1971).
24. *Possible Episomes in Eukaryotes.* Silvestri, L. G. (ed.) North-Holland Publishing Co. Amsterdam-London. (1973).
25. *The Mitochondria of Microorganisms.* Lloyd, D. Academic Press. 1974, p. 476.
26. Plattner, H. and Schatz, G. (1969). *Biochemistry,* 8, 339.

posed symbiosis occurred. This is meant to explain why mitochondrial superoxide dismutases are different from the cytosolic enzymes and tend to resemble the bacterial enzymes. If all this were true Fridovich is inclined to believe that **both** prokaryote and protoeukaryote already had aerobic life styles. The latter was not the anaerobic creature it is thought to be. This leaves the cause of the proposed symbiosis of the two unexplained.[27] For the moment many unsolved and important questions cloak the fascinating though superficial (so Lloyd[25]) similarities between bacteria and mitochondria. "Impressive as these similarities are, they do not prove an evolutionary origin of mitochondria from free-living organisms, since actually the reverse may be the case."[28] It may turn out that they are merely related by their inherent functions rather than by an evolutionary link of the kind proposed. This will be as hard to prove as it is to disprove.

Viruses have no membrane and do not have a metabolism apart from a living host cell. They tend to be set aside as irrelevant to the question of the origin of cellular life. In fact their developed form of intracellular parasitism mark them as evolutionarily late in origin, being themselves possibly derived from organelles.

PRE-CELLULAR TO CELLULAR

*"After all, primitive systems able to evolve indefinitely through natural selection **should** be fairly easy to make: nature produced at least one without natural selection, and nature is less competent than we are at making machinery abiologically. If we have so far failed to make 'life' in this sense, it is, I think, because we have been trying to climb the wrong evolutionary tree."*

A. G. Cairns-Smith (1975)[29]

27. Fridovich, I. (1974) in *Horizons in Biochemistry and Biophysics.* Quagliariello, E. and Palmieri, F. (eds.). Addison-Wesley Publishing Co. Reading, Massachusetts.
28. Schatz, G. (1970) in *Membranes of Mitochondria and Chloroplasts.* Racker, E. (ed.) Van Nostrand Reinhold Co., p. 251.
29. Cairns-Smith, A. G. (1975) *Proc. R. Soc. Lond. B.* **189**, 249.

At one stage in the history of the earth the cell arose, marking the boundary between chemical and biological evolution. What was the first cell like and what are the experimental grounds for postulating any definite line of "cellular" development? The picture emerges, though somewhat murky, of an early metabolising unit equivalent to the "eobiont" of Pirie,[30] the "protobiont" of Oparin[31] or the CITROENS of Orgel (Complex Information-Transforming Reproducing Objects that Evolve by Natural Selections).[32] To Cairns-Smith the idea of "life" is not even a unit but an open system consisting of mineral crystals able to catalyse the formation of sugars. He speaks of "slurry-gels constituting these early life systems" and shortly invests them with the exalted title "sugar-containing phenotypes"![33] We begin to feel that a masterly semantic and ideological sleight-of-hand has been performed. A certain vagueness is evident at this juncture because the eobiont cannot be truly living in the conventional sense (p. 127). It is, after all, in the process of acquiring a regular mechanism for metabolism and proliferation. The intrinsic difficulties that challenge scientists here, and how they try to understand them, are lucidly discussed by Pattee[34] and Hanson.[35] It is as unedifying to label these difficulties "hopelessly incomprehensible" as it is to delude oneself that they are of a minor nature. In most texts on the origin of life (including this one!) it is not surprising to meet with circumlocution in various guises just at this crucial point of the discussion. One other point is worthy of note, though. The thinking and experimentation in the field of life's beginnings has been dominated by the "heterotroph hypothesis." This requires the pre-existence

30. Pirie, N. W. (1953) *Discovery*, 14, 238.
31. Oparin, A. I. (1965). *Adv. in Enzymol.* 27, 347.
32. *The Origins of Life*. Orgel, L. E. Chapman and Hall Ltd. London (1973). p. 193.
33. Ref. 29, p. 262.
34. Pattee, H. H. (1965). *Adv. in Enzymol.*, 27, 381.
35. Hanson, E. D. (1966) *Quart. Rev. Biol.*, 41, 1.

of all the organic and inorganic compounds necessary to
the functioning of a cell. Of this Keosian noted, "But the
simplest heterotrophic cell is an intricate structural and
metabolic unit of harmoniously coordinated parts and
chemical pathways. Its spontaneous assembly out of the
environment, granting the unlikely simultaneous presence
together of all the parts, is not a believable possibility."
But Keosian's alternative, "the autotrophic hypothesis," is
hardly more believable![36]

We must now briefly look at the experimental findings
relating to the formation of cell-like structures. Fox and his
co-workers have synthesised proteinoid polymers, rich in
aspartic and glutamic acids, which, in aqueous solutions,
become stable microspheres.[37] These microspheres exhibit interesting phenomena such as "budding," and
transferring discrete "endoparticles" from one sphere to
another and weak enzymatic properties, [38,39] Under light
and electron microscopy double layers are seen resembling those of a cell. Although no catalytic activity is
detected in the membranes, the incorporation of Zn^{2+} invested them with ATPase properties. In the discussion
following Fox's paper several points came up for comment.[37] One point concerned the thickness of the membrane compared with that of the living cell. It is 10-20
times thicker than a biological membrane. Another point
was that the synthetic sequences of amino acids ➤
proteinoid ➤ microspheres required drastic changes
in geophysical conditions in passing from one stage to the

---

36. Keosian, J. (1974) in *The Origin of Life and Evolutionary
    Biochemistry*. Dose, K., Fox, S. W., Deborin, G. A. and Pavlov-
    skaya, T. E. (eds.) Plenum Press. New York and London. p. 221.
37. Fox. S. W. (1965). in *The Origins of Prebiological Systems*. Fox, S.
    W. (ed.) Academic Press. p. 361.
38. Fox, S. W. (1971). in *Prebiotic and Biochemical Evolution*. Kimball,
    A. P. and Oro', J. (eds.). North-Holland Publishing Co. Amsterdam-
    London. p. 8.
39. Hsu, L. L. and Fox, S. W. (1976). *Biosystems*, 8, 89.

other. This objection has been partly overcome by the synthesis of microspheres from proteinoid at low temperatures. Bernal has expressed his doubts over the relevance of proteinoid microspheres to the problem of the origin of life.[40] In Oparin's opinion, Fox's micro- spheres are not a promising lead because their static struc- ture may create difficulties when it comes to converting them into dynamic systems.[41] He favours the use of coacervate drops which are formed when colloidal par- ticles, previously distributed uniformly in solution, are, under certain conditions, collected in one place. (Latin *acervus*—a heap or pile). Coacervate drops can be formed from two or more components. The colloid-rich fraction is called the coacervate and the colloid-poor medium the equilibrium liquid. Combinations of protein-carbohy- drate, protein-protein, protein-nucleic acid, protein-car- bohydrate-nucleic acid, and protein-lipid mixtures have been successfully used.

Coacervate droplets contain a considerable amount of solvent, are immiscible with the liquid from which they arise and with which they are in equilibrium. Important as cell models, they can concentrate highly polymerised substances from very dilute solutions and allow exchange of materials with the medium in which they are dispersed. Simple "metabolic" experiments with enzymes carried out on coacervate droplets will be discussed in a subse- quent section on thermodynamics. It is also noted that coacervate droplets exist only within certain well-defined physico-chemical limits, and have nothing in the nature of a limiting membrane. This allows a dynamic interaction with the medium such as increasing their volumes by the acquisition of material from the medium.

Though vacuoles may be seen within the droplets, they are generally structureless. This is one reason why Bernal

----

40. Ref. 6, p. 125.
41. *Genesis and Evolutionary Development of Life.* Oparin, A. I. Academic Press. (1968). p. 105.

considers coacervates as being not directly relevant to the problem of the origin of life; the other reason is that their method of formation implies the pre-existence of complicated polymer molecules.[42] In his view they were later developments in the evolution of life. Bernal considers that life emerged at the point coinciding with the development of a mechanism for the precise replication of molecules.[43] It is curious that Paecht-Horowitz has objected to the use of Oparin's coacervate model for the very reason that Oparin dislikes Fox's proteinoid microsphere. A state of equilibrium is soon set up between the coacervate droplet and the surrounding medium unless a suitable catalyst is deliberately incorporated.[44] Marcel Florkin also gives the coacervate theory of the origin of life short shrift because he believes that Fox's proteinoid spherules are a better alternative.[45]

Membranes are such essential components of living systems that only a greater understanding of their ultrastructure will allow realistic cell models to be set up.[13,46,47] Already important facts on the physiological principles underlying molecular organisation have accrued from work carried out with artificial phospholipid membranes, while chemical analysis of isolated biological membranes, particularly those of red-cells and bacteria, have yielded useful information.

---

42. Ref. 6, p. 126.
43. Ref. 6, p. 170-171.
44. Paecht-Horowitz, M. (1973) *Angew. Chemie. Internat. Edit.* 12, 349.
45. Florkin, M. (1975). in *Comprehensive Biochemistry.* Florkin, M. and Stotz, E. H. (eds.) Elsevier Scientific Publishing Co. Vol 29B, p. 231.
46. *Membranes—Structure and Function.* Willanueva, J. R. and Ponz, F. Academic Press. (1970).
47. a. Hendler, R. W. (1971). *Physio. Revs.,* 51, 66.
    b. Kaplan, D. M. and Criddle, R. S. (1971) *Physio. Revs., 51,* 249.

THE "ALL-OR-NONE" PRINCIPLE

In considering cell structure and function there is an important principle of "all-or-none." The principle of continuity (p. 64) is its logical extension in the dimension of time. The principle may be illustrated in this way. The cell can be regarded as a highly complex and integrated metabolic machine. To what extent can the component parts be deleted or altered without a derangement in total function? What is the absolute minimum number of cellular components (organelles, enzymes, proteins, nucleic acids, other organic and inorganic material) that would constitute a living cell? One answer is that it depends on the stage of cellular evolution that one has in mind. A more primitive cell, by definition, would presumably require less metabolic "furniture" than its more advanced descendant. In the grand tradition of evolutionary logic (random mutation followed by selection of enhanced reproductive capacity) this line of reasoning seems acceptable. But we need to remember that this reasoning has been extrapolated "backward" from observations made on organisms which answer all the criteria of being "living."

Dobzhansky has entered a plea for a more careful use of the words "natural selection." "Natural selection is differential reproduction, organism perpetuation. In order to have natural selection you have to have self-reproduction or self-replication and at least two distinct self-replicating units or entities . . . . Prebiological natural selection is a contradiction of terms."[48] In contrast, Oparin has argued along the following lines. "All sorts of changes and shifts in the protobionts could have occurred during their growth and disintegration, especially if the environmental conditions changed. However, all this taken together would lead to the appearance of a peculiar type of prebiological 'natural selection' which predetermined the

---

48. *Ref. 37, p. 310.*

further evolution of protobionts toward the formation of primary living things."[49] In another paper Oparin commented, rather hopefully, "In the protobionts, polymerisation of amino acids could certainly take place giving rise to those combinations of residues that were able to play the role of enzymes."[50] Here as elsewhere one cannot have one's cake and eat it. For we have seen that the asymmetric synthesis of proteins still remains unsolved at this juncture. The closest experimental evidence having any bearing on the problem required that quartz or some other mineral should play a part in such a synthesis (p. 144). These minerals would be located outside the protobionts (as in Cairns-Smith's model[29]).

The experimental basis of Oparin's statement is probably based on observations of the behaviour of coacervates to which "suitable catalysts" have been incorporated. These catalysts include chlorophyll, bacterial oxidoreductase, phosphorylase, and α-amylase. Oparin has also theorised that "the protobionts which originate in the primeval broth possessed (just as our coacervate models do) the primeval metabolism reactions (oxidation-reduction, coupling, and polymerisation)." This is an enormous leap not warranted by the experimental facts presently available. The tacit assumption is that a proteinoid spherule or coacervate droplet endowed with two, or even three, catalytic functions, somehow propitiously related in a metabolic sense, should have survived, reproduced its kind, and improved itself. This assumption should be capable of experimental verification, such as noting the long-term effects on a population of coacervate droplets under the very best conditions conceivable to see if anything resembling primitive metabolic cycles or replication will appear.

---

49. Ref. 31, p. 371.
50. Oparin, A. I. (1972) in Exobiology. Ponnamperuma, C. (ed.) North-Holland Publishing Co. Amsterdam-London. p. 1.

METABOLIC COMPLEXITY

In the living cell, enzymes function in concert such that the product of one enzyme becomes the substrate of another. The concept of enzymes functionally linked as chains and cycles is commonplace biochemical knowledge. But it is knowledge won by the meticulous labours of many biochemists for over half a century. The continuing discovery of new enzymes and previously unsuspected regulatory links in metabolic pathways is ample testimony to the fact that much more remains to occupy biochemists in the years to come. There has been accumulating evidence that enzymes which act sequentially may also be spatially close to each other in the living cell. This relationship is often disrupted when the cell is broken up. As early as 1940, referring to the succinate dehydrogenase-cytochrome system, Keilin and Hartree wrote, "The activity of this system depends not only on the properties of the individual components but also on those of the colloidal protein particles to which they are more or less intimately bound. It is conceivable that each of the colloidal particles acts as a support for the complete system and thus assures the mutual accessibility of its components."[51] The metabolic integration of enzymes and of structurally organised enzyme systems and their properties has been discussed at various times. The subject has been reviewed recently by Ginsburg and Stadtman. "It has become increasingly clear that most intracellular enzyme systems may be highly organised by means of a tight or loose association with the particulate portions of the cell."[52]

It has been shown that, in some systems, such as the fatty acid synthetase from yeast and the arom aggregate from fungi, the dissociated complexes have no enzymatic ac-

---

51. Keilin, D. and Hartree, E. F. (1940). *Proc. Roy. Soc.* (Lond.) Series B. 129, 277.
52. Ginsburg, A. and Stadtman, E. R. (1970). *Ann. Rev. Biochem.* 39, 727.

tivity. Recently a membrane enzyme system—the galactosyl transferase system of Salmonella typhimurium—was successfully reassembled in vitro from the purified components. Lipopolysaccharide, phosphatidyl ethanolamine, and enzyme protein were all required for the restoration of function.[53,54] In vitro evidence has also been presented for a non-catalytic carrier protein which originates in the endoplasmic reticulum and which appears essential for cholesterol biosynthesis. The carrier binds the substrate and makes it reactive to the sterol synthesising enzyme. It also possibly acts as a transport system for cholesterol in the cell.[55] Moreover, ATP generation that is linked to the respiratory chain appears to be obligatorily associated with membranous structures. The biosyntheses of cell-wall mucopeptide and lipopolysaccharides in microorganisms are also functions of membranes.

Assemblies of protein molecules represent a fundamental level of biological organisation. The multi-enzyme assembly has clear advantages in the way of the minimum transit time for substrate molecules, effective separation of biosynthetic and degradative pathways when these are potentially competitive and the possibility of group regulation by protein-protein interaction. Were these complexes selected in the course of evolution for these and other advantages? It would appear that they were. The question then becomes, "How was this achieved?" The loss of activity of some enzyme systems apart from the membranes which lodge them pose an intriguing problem as to how such systems evolved.

53. Romeo, D., Girard, A., and Rothfield, L. (1970). *J. Mol. Biol.,* 53, 475.
54. Romeo, D., Hinckley, A., and Rothfield, L. (1970). *J. Mol. Biol.,* 53, 491.
55. Scallen, T. J., Schuster, M. W., and Dhar, A. K. (1971). *J. Mol. Biol.,* 246, 224.

METABOLIC DEVELOPMENT

A parallel situation is met in the development of intermediary metabolism and its regulation.[29,35,56-61,63-65]

Horowitz Model

Horowitz proposed that biosynthetic pathways grew by a process of "retrograde evolution,"[56] a process which Miller and Orgel[65] discuss in some detail. When a nutrient was exhausted by an organism, others of its kind were selected which were able to manufacture the nutrient from an immediate precursor, presumably because these organisms had the necessary enzyme(s). Suppose that a pathway $A \rightarrow B \rightarrow C \rightarrow D \rightarrow E$ exists in an ancient organism. When the supply of E is exhausted the organism evolves an enzyme to make E from D. In turn, D to A runs out and an opportunity is given to the organism to develop a metabolic sequence. Objections to Horowitz's scheme have been raised by both Yĉas[63] and Cairns-Smith.[29] There must be a stock-pile of necessary intermediates available in the environment the production of which obligingly disappears one by one in sequence. Metabolic intermediates in general have short half-lives.

56. Horowitz, N. H. (1945). *Proc. Natl. Acad. Sci.* (Wash.) 31, 153.
57. Eakin, R. E. (1963) *Proc. Natl. Acad. Sci.* (Wash.) 49, 360.
58. Nordone, R. M. (1968) in *Genetics, Development, and Evolution.* Nardone, R. M. (ed.) Catholic University of America Press. Washington, D. C. p. 45.
59. Allen, G. (1957) *Amer. Natur.* 91, 65.
60. Allen, G. (1970) *Persp. in Biol. and Med.,* 14, 109.
61. Lipmann, F. (1965) ref. 37, p. 259.
62. Siu, P. M. L. and Wood, H. G. (1962). *J. Biol. Chem.* 237, 3044.
63. Yĉas, M. (1974) *J. Theoret. Biol.* 44, 145.

64. Buvet, R. (1974) in *The Origins of Life and Evolutionary Biochemistry.* Dose, K., Fox, S. W., Deborin, G. A., and Pavlovskaya, T. E. (eds.) Plenum Press. New York and London. p. 41.
65. *The Origins of Life on the Earth.* Miller, S. L. and Orgel, L. E. Prentice-Hall, Inc., Englewood Cliffs, New Jersey. (1974). p. 186.

Eakin Model

Eakin has built upon the dehydration of glycerate-2-phosphate to form an unstable enol pyruvic acid and a high-energy reactive anhydride of phosphoric acid.[57] Around this core reaction are added related reactions in step-wise fashion. For instance, some glycerol 2,3 phosphate may be produced from glycerol phosphate. As the diphosphate primes the reaction that converts glycerol-3-phosphate to glycerol-2-phosphate in the modern cell, through phosphoglycerate 2,3 mutase, its appearance is postulated to have led to the annexing of this conversion to the initial reaction. Two assumptions are made: (1) that the functional ancestors like ADP existed, capable of accepting and donating phosphate groups, and (2) these organic co-factors functioned without enzyme proteins. An inspection of the first of Eakin's series of postulated reactions renders the entire scheme highly unrealistic. This is the conversion of triosephosphate (glycerol-2-phosphate) into pyruvate. In the cell this is accomplished in two steps. The first of these is performed by an enzyme enolase:

$$
\begin{array}{ccc}
\text{COO}^- & & \text{COO}^- \\
| & \xrightarrow{\quad H_2O \quad} & | \\
H-C-OPO_3^{2-} & \rightleftharpoons & C-OPO_3^{2-} \\
| & & \| \\
CH_2OH & & CH_2 \\
\end{array}
$$

2-phospho-D-glycerate   **phospho-enol-pyruvate**

and is completed by the phosphorylation of ADP, catalysed by pyruvate kinase.

$$\begin{array}{c} COO^- \\ | \\ C-OPO_3^{2-} \\ || \\ CH_2 \end{array} + ADP^{3-} \xrightarrow{\quad Mg^{2+}\quad} ATP^{4-} + \begin{array}{c} COO^- \\ | \\ C=O \\ | \\ CH_3 \end{array}$$

It is hard to visualise that the foregoing conversion, which normally involves two enzymes and cofactors, took place with the aid of clays as catalysts.

Allen Model

Allen had earlier proposed the reflexively catalytic system, where a product of a series of reactions catalyses an earlier reaction, thus leading to the formation of more of itself.[59] Side reactions producing isomers of the essential compounds provide a basis for an evolution analogous to that provided by genes. These ideas have been reformulated as the "bion hypothesis."[60] To quote the central hypothesis, "The first regular self-replication of ordered linear polymers on the earth was preceded by a period of evolution by natural selection among simpler organic molecules that did not serve as templates but reproduced by promoting other reactions critical for their own synthesis." A bion is a reflexive catalytic series of reactions. Operating together in one system, several bions could mainfest the basic properties of life. With Allen, Eakin argues that self-copying biopolymers need not enter their concepts of the early stages of chemical evolution.

Both Allen and Eakin face the difficulty of postulating credible sequences of reactions to clothe their conceptual framework. If this could be done it would provide guidelines for experimental work. How useful were these reactions outside a limiting membrane of a cell? When cell membranes were acquired were they permeable to some or all the essential metabolites, especially in the case of phosphorylated and other highly polar compounds? Were the sequential reactions of the kind described more likely to produce catalytic rather than inhibitory molecules? In other words, were inhibitory reflexive systems (for example, via competitive inhibition) more or less likely outcomes than catalytic systems?

Lipmann Model

Fritz Lipmann's proposals are based on the availability of pyrophosphate (energy-carrier) and the activation of hydrogen by catalysts of the ferredoxin variety (then newly-discovered).[61] Further stimulation was provided by the discovery of a primary reaction of CO_2 fixation.[62] The enzyme was isolated from Propionibacterium shermanii and named phosphoenolpyruvate carboxytransphosphorylase—to indicate the dual function of CO_2 fixation and the transfer of phosphate to pyrophosphate or phosphoenolpyruvate (PEP).

Ferredoxins fo the 8Fe + 8S variety are now known to possess 8 invariant cysteine positions and some microorganisms have 50% of amino acid residues in common. It is unlikely that ferredoxins were the earliest proteins. It is also difficult to see how fixation of CO_2 can proceed to more complex carbon structures. Lipmann's reasoning is based largely on biochemical reactions now existing. To assume that a 2-carbon unit like acetate will become the ancestor of fats and lipids is being too facile.

Yĉas Model

Strictly speaking, the Yĉas model is not relevant to a discussion of the origin of metabolic pathways, but to their further development.[63] Like Lipmann, Yĉas argues backward from contemporary enzyme systems. In essence he imagines that the earlier enzymes must be ones with broad specificity in order that pathways could evolve while the viability of the cell is maintained.

Cairns-Smith Model

This model requires an initially open system which maintains a super-saturated solution of crystals.[29] Selection favours defect patterns that encourage rapid growth. These defects are propagated by internal printing during crystal growth. The hypothesis further requires that these defects should **accurately** propagate themselves. Herein lies the beginnings of a crystal gene system. If an immense set of possible patterns is rapidly propagating and interacting within itself it is hard to see how accuracy, presumably in a very small subset, could favour the establishment of a mineral gene. Next it is required that the mineral gene catalyse a formose-type reaction to produce sugars from formaldehyde. What selective advantage this has is anybody's guess. Cairns-Smith and Walker reason that this sugary jam confers distinct survival value on their system.[66] The "next long stage" of evolution is the selection of "formose phenotypes" which make the types of sugars the "organism" **needs**. The trend of evolution of such an "organism" could include the Lipmann sequence of events, along with the hidden assumptions subsumed by that scheme.

All the models outlined suffer severe deficiencies of which their authors are only too well aware. Perhaps the greatest contribution to this area of enquiry will come from the study of bacterial enzyme systems. Hegeman and Rosenberg have outlined two approaches to this study.[67] The descriptive approach is aimed at obtaining taxonomic and evolutionary information and concerns itself with the perpetuation, dissemination, and recombination of enzymatic functions. A frequent dilemma is that a distinction cannot be made between the processes of convergent and divergent evolution that may act in different ways to produce similar results.

The experimental approach is concerned with the origin, integration, and uses of new enzymatic function. Work on mutants of Aerobacter aerogenes capable of

---

66. Cairns-Smith, A. G. and Walker, G. L. (1974) *Biosystems 5*, 173.
67. *Hegeman, G. D. and Rosenberg, S. L. (1970) Ann. Rev. Microbiol.*, 24, 429.

utilising xylitol as a novel carbon source has shown that genes, belonging to different metabolic systems, can be mobilised to serve a new biochemical pathway by appropriate mutations.[68] Mutations that confer the ability to synthesise constitutively an originally inducible enzyme or group of enzymes appear to be the most commonly observed mechanism by which bacteria are enabled to grow on a novel substrate. This lends some weight to Horowitz's proposal for a retrograde evolution of metabolic pathways.

The duplication of genes is an unlikely mechanism for the evolution of metabolic systems, although it could possibly account for the appearance of a series of proteins with homologous functions, such as myoglobin, various sub-units of haemoglobin, haptoglobins, and transferrins. The duplication of a chromosomal segment being a random event, cannot respond to environmental demands, nor create novelty. Certainly if enzymes of a metabolic pathway arise from each other they will display some measure of similarity in their amino acid sequences or immunological behaviour. There has also been renewed interest in the mechanisms behind the phenomenon of protein polymorphisms. One view, is that point mutations are mainly neutral to selection. Random drift of these neutral mutations in finite populations are said to account for the observed protein polymorphisms.[69,70] One consequence of this will be a greater heterogeneity in the amino acid sequences of proteins than allowed for previously.

THERMODYNAMICS AND THE CELL

Thermodynamics is a branch of physics that emphasises the application of the concept of energy, its conservation, and how energy can change its form. The use of ther-

---

68. Wu, T. T., Lin, E. C. C., and Tanaka, S. (1968). *J. Bact.,* 96, 447.
69. Kimura, M. (1968). *Nature,* 217, 624.
70. Kimura, M. and Ohta, T. (1971). *Nature,* 229, 467.

modynamics in biological systems forms the core of biophysics. The treatment of living systems requires simplifying assumptions since molecules are complex and are present in a multi-component system, a system being the collection of matter under study.

Thermodynamics concern finite systems of which two main types are defined—open and closed. An example of a closed system is a chemical reaction in a test tube. Heat may be generated and this is lost to the environment. After a while a thermodynamic equilibrium is reached at which point entropy (disorder) is maximum. No matter has entered the system. A living organism is an open system in that there is an interchange both of energy and matter with the environment. That is, the reactants are fed into an organism and the products are removed, so that the organism reaches a steady state. All the time the viable organism is creating order out of disorder through metabolism and biosynthesis. And it propagates that order by self-replication.

The second law of classical thermodynamics carries the concept that all spontaneous processes tend toward equilibrium. Once a system is at equilibrium no useful work can be obtained. It used to be thought that living things do not obey the second law until it was realised that they are open systems. Such systems invariably consist of a variety of inter-linked chemical processes which may be linear but are often branched. The processes are in steady state rather than in equilibrium and entropy is produced at a minimum rate. Being in non-equilibrium they can be subjected to metabolic regulation. Furthermore an open system provides the cell with an extended time scale with the possibility of development. The properties of the system reach a constant level during maturity. Non-equilibrium or irreversible thermodynamics, as a branch of classic thermodynamics, has developed since the 1920s to deal with these phenomena. This has led to helpful concepts in dealing with what the term "living" really means but, as Mora has pointed out, "it still remains to be explained why living units operate as irreversible process so that entropy content decreases **invariably** in the growing state, and why they revert immediately at death to the increase of entropy."[71]

As the understanding of living things in terms of systems which are in non-equilibrium begins to mature several interesting properties of such systems have emerged. Denbigh has called attention to the fact that the steady state at which entropy production is at minimum rate will only be possible if the system is close to equilibrium, which most biological processes are not.[72] Biological processes are controlled by kinetic parameters and not by their thermodynamic complexion alone. This is a point not often appreciated.[73] Thus the synthesis of a compound if efficiently catalysed will proceed in spite of an unfavourable equilibrium constant provided (1) that the products are effectively removed and (2) the standard free energy change associated with the reaction is not too largely positive.

PROTOTYPES OF THE LIVING CELL

An examination of the origin of life must go beyond a formulation of the conditions necessary for the spontaneous generation of organic molecules. Various models have been offered as the progenitors of the living cell. These include proteinoid spherules and coacervate droplets. Oparin has reviewed his experimental evidence for the coacervate droplet as a simple "cell" functioning as a steady state system.[74] For instance, glucose-1-phosphate is made to diffuse into a coacervate droplet where a phosphorylase polymerises it to starch, releasing inorganic phosphate. If maltase is also present in the droplet maltose (a disaccharide) is cleaved from the ends of the starch chains and would diffuse into the medium.

Insofar as the system is a method to trap phosphorylase

71. Mora, P. Ref. 37, p. 43.
72. Denbigh, G. K. (1952). *Trans. Faraday Soc.* 48, 389.
73. Banks, B. E. C. and Vernon, C. A. (1970). *J. Theoret. Biol.* 29, 301.
74. Ref. 41, p. 101-126.

and maltase in gum arabic droplets, presumably by ionic repulsion from the negatively charged histone solution, the system is ingenious. The starch, of course, cannot diffuse out. The increase of entropy due to diffusional flow of substrates into the droplets may be sufficient to compensate for the entropy decrease of the synthesis of the starch polymer.[75] But it must be remembered that whether the enzymes are free or locked in a coacervate, the system as a whole will reach the same thermodynamic equilibrium after some time. A living organism, although an open system in steady state, can react to a stimulus (such as an increase in the substrate concentration of the surrounding medium) by resisting in such a manner that its own steady state may be assumed after a time interval, with possibilities of variety in the transitional stages between one steady level and another. These features, so conspicuous in living systems, are the hypothetical end-products of Oparin's "protobionts" after a long evolutionary history. The course of this development remains to be elucidated.

It is of interest to note that a simple open system containing a reversible chemical reaction such as Oparin's[76] is capable of various types of almost "lifelike behaviour." When the system passes from one steady state to another the transition stages include the possibilities of "overshoot" and "false starts."[77] In more elaborate systems with two reversible reactions in tandem, oscillation may occur though they cannot be prolonged indefinitely. Open systems kinetics are therefore likely to provide suitable bases for the investigation of physiological processes which they imitate. A number of kinetic and thermodynamic criteria for the occurrence of oscillatory phenomena in some biochemical systems has been

75. Reiner, J. M. and Spiegelman, S. (1945). *J. Physic. Chem.* 49, 81.
76. Ref. 41, p. 117.
77. Bray, G. H. and White, K. (1966). *Kinetics and Thermodynamics in Biochemistry,* J & A Churchill Ltd. p. 201.

reviewed recently.[78-80]

It is fitting to close this section with a quotation from Ponnamperuma. "There is an extensive literature dealing with the accumulation of various solutions of organic matter and the resulting cell-like structures. However, the leap from morphology to function is fraught with danger, especially when we consider entities of several billion years ago."[81]

78. Hess, B. and Boitevx, A. (1971). *Ann. Rev. Biochem.* 40, 237.

79. Prigogine, I. and Babloyantz, A. (1971). in *Chemical Evolution and the Origin of Life.* Buvet, R. and Ponnamperuma, C. (eds.) North Holland Publishing co. p. 29.

80. Rubin, A. B. (1974) in *The Origin of Life and Evolutionary Biochemistry.* Dose, K., Fox, S. W., Deborin, G. A., and Pavlovskaya, T. E. (eds.) Plenum Press. New York and London. p. 417.

81. *The Origins of Life.* Ponnamperuma, C. Thames and Hudson, London. (1972). p. 102.

Chapter 7

The Role of Adenosine Triphosphate

INTRODUCTION

Adenosine triphosphate (ATP) is a source of readily available chemical energy. Its central position in the ordinary life processes—the active transport of ions and metabolites across cell membranes, the biosynthesis of macromolecules, muscular contraction—is apparent even to cursory enquiry. ATP donates its phosphate group with the release of a standard free energy ($\Delta G°$) of about 7 kcal. The exact value of the $\Delta G°$ is in some dispute, but the fact remains that the hydrolysis of ATP is exergonic or energy-releasing, enabling it to "drive" chemical reactions that are energetically unfavourable. It is of interest to note that ATP is among the list of substances looked for in interplanetary probes.[1,2] Refinements in instrumentation and biochemistry make it possible to detect the ATP of approximately 200 Escherichia coli or that of one yeast cell.

STRUCTURE

ATP is quite stable in a chemical sense (Fig. 18). The last two phosphate groups are only hydrolysed in 1 N HC1 for 7 minutes. The energy resides not in the phosphate bond *per se,* but in the structural features of the compound. The decreased electrical stress in the molecule of adenosine diphosphate (ADP) formed by the removal of a terminal phosphate of ATP and the stabilisation of ADP as resonance hybrids contribute to the large negative standard energy of hydrolysis. Alternative high energy bonds have been proposed. The experimental evidence shows that arsenate, for instance, though it can substitute for phosphate in enzymatic reactions, tends to disrupt the reaction and act as an energy leak.

---

1. Vishniac, W., Atwood, K. C., Bock, R. M., Gaffron, H., Jukes, T. H., McLaren, A.D., Sagan, C., and Spinrad, H. (1966). in *Biology and the Exploration of Mars.* Pittendrigh, C. S., Vishniac, W., and Pearman, J. P. T. (eds.). Natl. Acad. Sci., Natl. Res. Council, Washington, D.C. p. 229-242.
2. Levin, C. V., Clendenning, J. R., Chapelle, E. W., Heim, A. H., and Rocek, E. (1964) *Bioscience,* 14, 37.

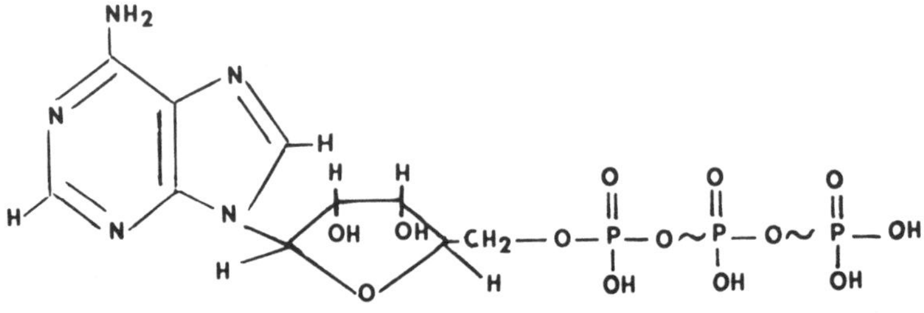

Figure 18. The structural formula of ATP. (∼) signifies a high energy phosphate bond.

Photosynthetic pigments convert light energy to chemical energy in the green cells of higher plants, certain algae, and bacteria. The higher animals, most micro-organisms, and non-photosynthetic plant cells, utilise the energy of oxidation-reduction reactions carried out on electron donors such as glucose. The metabolic pathways, so ably unravelled since the first half of the present century, interlock with ATP production at several points.

LABORATORY SYNTHESIS OF ATP

The laboratory synthesis of various nucleosides and nucleotides has been described in an earlier section (p. 39). The acknowledged centrality of ATP in energy metabolism has invested the finding of this compound in laboratory "soups" with an importance and mystique which, we shall argue, is misplaced.

Adenosine may be generated by irradiating dilute solutions of adenine, ribose (or deoxyribose), and $(NH_4)H_2PO_4$ or NaCN.[3,4] By treating adenosine with a rather unstable phosphorylating agent, polymetaphosphate ethyl ester, and irradiating with UV light, ADP, ATP can be detected. The possibility that solar energy can be stored in the form

3. Ponnamperuma, C., Sagan, C., and Marmar, R. (1963) *Nature,* 199, 222.
4. Ponnamperuma, C. and Kirk, P. (1964) *Nature,* 203, 400.

of ATP is suggested by the work of several investigators. Phosphorylation of ADP to yield ATP was noted when iron porphyrin, phosphate, imidazole, and ADP (or AMP) were irradiated in the presence of oxygen in a non-aqueous medium. The intermediate was identified as phospho-imidazole, which converted ADP to ATP.[5]

THE PRIMITIVE SYNTHESIS OF
HIGH ENERGY PHOSPHATE BONDS

It has been postulated that life arose and evolved only when the protobionts were capable of coupling the energy of dehydrogenation to the necessary synthesis of all those compounds that were required for replication. The first energy-trapping reaction has been proposed as one involving the pyrophosphate bond.

$$AH_2 + B + P \longrightarrow A + BH_2 + \sim P$$

As more AH_2 was oxidised, the protobionts relied on less reduced compounds for coupled oxidation-reduction reactions, so that subsequent dehydration and energy coupling may proceed as follows.

$$BH_2 + C + P \longrightarrow B + CH_2 + \sim P$$

This process of energy trapping was crucial. But such a complicated molecule as ATP was unlikely to have been the first energy-rich compound as pyrophosphates may have been initially important.[6]

Though it stretches one's credulity it has also been proposed that the primordial cell might have possibly developed (by natural selection, of course) a simple electron transport system from pyridine nucleotides to

---

5. Brinigar, W. S., Knaff, D. B., and Wang, J. H. (1967) *Biochemistry*, 6, 36.

6. De Ley, J. (1975) *Proc. R. Soc. Lond. B.* 189, 235.

flavoprotein to cytochrome to O_2.[7] "The next major event was the appearance of an integrated electron transport chain endowed with respiratory control, hence the capacity for oxidative phosphorylation. In present day organisms this event invariably requires the presence of a membrane system. So the development of a lipid-containing membrane appears to have been a prerequisite for this gigantic leap." (!) Singer pays tribute to the endosymbiotic theory of the origin of mitochondria but concedes, "it does not answer the central question of the origin of the assembly of the respiratory chain."[8] In discussions on bioenergetic evolution Broda outlines his arguments for the order of appearance of the major groups of ATP-generating processes.[9,10] Thus we have fermentators evolving to photo-organotrophs as a first stage up the ladder to oxidative phosphorylation. Neglecting for the moment the fact that fermentators may not have been the most primitive organisms we have to explain the genesis of complexity in photo-organotrophs such as the photosynthetic non-sulphur bacteria. Complexity that allows absorption of light energy by photosynthetic pigments, its conversion to ATP, and the integrated biosynthetic reactions leading from organic compounds to cell materials using chemical bond energy from light. The central question remains unanswered.

Though a simple system may be proposed for the primitive photosynthetic scheme of producing ATP, as given above, the fact remains that at present a profusion of theories testify to the lack of understanding in the crucial area of how ATP is being made by the modern organism.

7. Singer, T. P. (1971) in *Biochemical Evolution and the Origin of Life.* Schoffeniels, E. (ed.) North-Holland Publishing Co. p. 203.
8. Ref. 7, p. 219.
9. Ref. 7, p. 224.
10. Broda, E. in *Progress in Biophysics and Molecular Biology.* Butler, J. A. V. and Noble, D. (eds.) Pergamon Press, Oxford. 1971. Vol. 21, p. 209.

TABLE 6

Nature of Theory	Remarks	Refs.
Chemical Theories A chemical link exists between oxidation and phosphorylation via a "high-energy intermediate"	No such intermediate has been identified	11, 12, 13
Mechanical Coupling The mitochondrion, like a biochemical machine, undergoes reversible changes in shape when energised. The conformational changes are coupled to electron flow	Changes of shape in mitochondria are real and this is associated directly with ATP synthesis but the actual process is not specified	14, 15
Chemiosmotic Theory Electron transfer is coupled to the production of a potential difference between two sides of the mitochondrial membrane due to unequal distribution of H^+.	Current Theory includes a hypothetical "high-energy" anhydride precursor of ATP which has not been isolated.	16, 17

11. Chance, B. and Williams, G. R. (1959) *Adv. Enzymol.*, 17, 65.
12. Lehninger, A. L. (1965) *the Mitochondrion.* New York: W. A. Benjamin, Inc.
13. Slater, E. C. (1966) in *Flavins and Flavoproteins.* Elsevier, Amsterdam.
14. Green, D. E. and Maclenan, D. H. (1967) in *Metabolic Pathways* (ed.) Greenberg, D. Academic Press. Vol. 1, 3rd ed. p. 48.
15. Baum, H. (1968) *New Sci.*, 38, 460.
16. Mitchell, P. (1968) *Chemiosmotic Coupling and Energy Transduction.* Glynn Research Ltd. Bodmin.
17. Mitchell, P. (1973) in *Mechanisms in Bioenergetics.* Azzone, G. F., Ernster, L., Papa, S., Quagliariello, E., and Siliprandi, N. (ed.) Academic Press, New York and London. p. 177.

Various theories have been devised to account for the experimental observations of the effects of a variety of conditions and substances on oxidative phosphorylation. The main theories and their characteristics are summarised in Table 6.

Recent theories on ATP biosynthesis include those invoking proton flow[16] and a mechanical model.[18] The latter postulates a non-aqueous microenvironment where ADP and phosphoric acid are juxtaposed. This is created by an infolding of the mitochondrial membrane. ATPase then catalyses the direct esterification of ADP to ATP.[19]

The situation in the field of ATP biosynthesis is well summarised by Lehninger; "Today, 40 years after the discovery of ATP and almost 30 years after Lipmann proposed his theory of the central role of ATP in cellular energy transfer, we are still far from understanding how ATP is regenerated from ADP during electron transport, either in the mitochondrion or in the chloroplast."[20] This, in itself, poses no great barrier to an abiogenic view of the origin of life, provided one accepts that the widespread association of this compound with life forms today marked its "inevitable" appearance as an event of singular importance. The meaningful question is "How does the appearance of ATP favour the genesis of the primitive organism?" The first structures were not cells complete with membranes, nuclei, integrated metabolic pathways, and the property of self-replication. How did such "cells" utilise ATP? How is the chemical energy converted (transduced) into mechanical energy and vice versa within the primitive organism?

This is essentially a modern problem as well. The mechanism of synthesis of ATP is not simply a sort of reversal of the events of muscular contraction, during

18. Aldridge, W. N. and Rose, M. S. (1969) *FEBS Letters*, 4, 61.
19. Banks, B. E. C. and Vernon, C. A. (1970) *J. Theoret. Biol.*, 29, 301.
20. Lehninger, A. L. (1970) *Biochemistry*, Worth Publications, Inc., New York. p. 477.

which event ATP undergoes hydrolysis. It has become increasingly apparent that a multi-enzyme system catalyses the formation of ATP via oxidative phosphorylation and that this is done in close association with the inner membrane of mitochondria. The spatial relationships between the components of the system, the need for the separation of reactant molecules by a boundary (the hydrogen and hydroxyl ions of Mitchell's hypothesis, for instance) and the provision of both non-polar and polar microenvironments for reaction all require a membrane as a matrix.[21]

PHOSPHATE TRANSFERS, ENZYMES, AND ATP

Phosphate transfer, a widespread phenomenon in biological processes, need not involve ATP. An example of this is the reaction catalysed by the enzyme phosphoglycerate 2,3 mutase. In the main-stream of energy-transferring reactions, however, we find specific enzymes catalysing the transfer of phosphate groups from ATP to specific acceptors. For example, a large number of enzymes has been described which catalyse the phosphorylation of various sugars. An examination of the way one of these enzymes acts will demonstrate how, to a nicety, specificity of phosphorylation and the transfer of energy from one molecule (ATP) to another (a sugar) are both accommodated. The overall reaction catalysed by hexokinase is as follows:

β-D-GLUCOSE β-D-GLUCOSE-6-PHOSPHATE

---

21. *Membranes of Mitochondria and Chloroplasts.* Racker, E., (ed.) Van Nostrand Reinhold Co. 1970.

The mechanism proposed is one where an enzyme-bound glucose is phosphorylated by a complex of Mg^{2+} and ATP. A possible scheme is

$$\text{ATP}^{4-} \qquad\qquad\qquad \text{Mg-ATP}^{2-}$$

Mg-ATP^{2-} + Enzyme $\rightleftharpoons$ Mg-ATP-Enzyme

Mg-ATP-Enzyme + Glucose $\rightleftharpoons$ Glucose-6-phosphate + Mg-ADP-Enzyme

Mg-ADP-Enzyme $\rightleftharpoons$ ADP + Mg^{2+} + Enzyme

Apparently the catalytic niche on the enzyme can accommodate the intermediate (Mg-ATP-Glucose). Transfer of phosphate and energy has taken place in the active site provided by the enzyme protein. This feat is hard to imagine as occurring on the rather bland topology of a proteinoid spherule or a coacervate droplet, even though, by incorporating zinc, proteinoids may acquire the ability to hydrolyse ATP or pyrophosphate.[22] Oparin and his colleagues, in an ingenious experiment, allowed NADH$_2$ to diffuse into coacervate droplets containing NADH$_2$ dehydrogenase. The catalytic reduction of a dye was accompanied by the release of energy, which was dispersed mainly in the form of heat.[23]

Certain organelles or tissues such as flagella, cilia, and muscle undergo movements simultaneously with the hydrolysis of ATP to ADP and phosphate. In muscle ADP and inorganic phosphate are the products of an or-

---

22. Fox, S. W. (1965) in *The Origins of Prebiological Systems*. Fox, S. W. (ed.) Academic Press. p.361.

23. Oparin, A. I. (1968) *Genesis and Evolutionary Development of Life.* Fox, S. W. Academic Press. p. 361.

thophosphate cleavage of ATP.[24]

$$\text{Adenine-Ribose-P} \sim \text{P} \sim \text{P} \longrightarrow \text{Adenine-Ribose-P} \sim \text{P} + \text{Pi}$$

$$\Delta G^\circ = 8.61 \text{ kcal}$$

In many other reactions, however, ATP undergoes pyrophosphate cleavage.

$$\text{Adenine-Ribose-P} \sim \text{P} \sim \text{P} \longrightarrow \text{Adenine-Ribose-P} + \text{P} \sim \text{P}$$

The inorganic phyrophosphate is a high energy compound whose cleavage by the enzyme inorganic pyrophosphatase yields a further considerable amount of energy.

$$\text{P} \sim \text{P}_i^{3-} + \text{H}_2\text{O} \longrightarrow 2\text{P}_i^{2-} + \text{H}^+$$

The removal of pyrophosphate by such a coupled reaction is essential to the progression of the biosynthesis as this tends to shift the equilibrium of biosynthetic reactions to the right. The free energy of pyrophosphate hydrolysis is apparently lost but it ensures that synthesis is encouraged. This emphasises the point made earlier that, apart from the existence of enzymes and specialised tissues, the cleavage of high energy phosphate bonds appears to serve no direct function since the energy released is not utilisable. This would apply as well to the energy of oxidation-reduction reactions. As a matter of fact, heat is normally produced by the electron transport chain, thus dissipating part of its oxidation energy. This "uncoupling" of electron transport and phosphorylation is a physiologi-

---

24. A "warm" controversy on the energetics of muscle contraction in relation to ATP, and the place of thermodynamics in biology, ensued from an article by B. E. C. Banks in *Chem. Brit.* 5, 514 (1969). Articles by L. Pauling, A. F. Huxley, and D. Wilkie, and their rejoinders by C. A. Vernon, R. A. Ross, and Banks herself may be found in *Chem. Brit.*, 6, 468, 477 (1970) and 6, 539, 541 (1971).

cal feature of the mitochondria in brown adipose tissue. It serves to keep the animal warm. The important thing to note, however, is that this is not the main pathway of energy transfer in the respiratory chain. The design of mitochondrial form and function enables it to capture oxidation energy—a privilege denied to other structures of lesser sophistication.[25,26,27]

25. Palmer, J. M. and Hall, D. O. (1972) in *Progress in Biophysics and Molecular Biology*. Butler, J. A. V. and Noble, D. (eds.) Pergamon Press. Oxford. Vol. 24, p. 127.

26. *The Mechanism of Energy Transduction in Biological Systems*. Green, D. E. (ed.) Ann. N. Y. Acad. Sci. (1974). Vol. 227, p. 5-680.

27. *Energy Transducing Mechanisms*. Biochemistry Series One. Vol 3. Racker, E. (ed.) MTP International Review of Science. Butterworth University Park Press. (1974).

Chapter 8

The Philosophy of the Search for the Origin of Life

INTRODUCTION

Men from various scientific disciplines continue to be drawn toward trying to unravel the mystery of the origin of life. It is not easy to approach the study of origins in any field without some preconceived notions about what one may likely find. The interpretation of data is the product of analytical insight exercised within a complex matrix of one's own world view and the prevalent scientific climate. And whether or not a scientific fact is "proved" depends in part on the receptivity of the scientific community at a given time. The remarks of Dr. Francis Crick on motivations are also pertinent. In a buoyant mood ("when facts come in the door, vitalism flies out of the window") he said that the motivation of many people who have entered molecular biology from physics and chemistry has been their desire to disprove vitalism. He continues, "Indeed, while on the subject of motivation, it would be of interest for somebody to inquire into the religious faith of these various writers. I have a strong suspicion that it is the Christians, and the Catholics in particular, who write as vitalists, and it is the agnostics and atheists who are the antivitalists. Whether this is widely true I must confess I do not know."[1]

Scientists have expressed on various occasions their philosophy on the origin of life and of evolution. Inspiration may sometimes be drawn from unexpected sources. Thus Oparin brings in dialectical materialism to account for the fact that matter is in constant motion.[2] He also sees new forms arising as part of "the process of development of matter." This is hardly self-explanatory. It is interesting to note that Bernal also refers to the ideas of Engels and Marx when writing on the influence of contemporary

---

1. Crick, F. (1966) of *Molecules and Men*. University of Edinburgh Press. p. 25.
2. Oparin, A. I. (1968). *Genesis and Evolutionary Development of Life*. Academic Press. p. 3

thought on the discussion on the origins of life.[3]

There is more beyond the fascination of experiment and conjecture. Indeed, for some, the quest for the origin of life merges into a quest for the meaning of life. In concluding his discussion of chemical evolution Calvin remarked, "What is the reason for this pursuit, and where can it lead? Perhaps it can be best summarised by man's need to search for significances, in his own life, and in life itself."[4] These sentiments are echoed by Bernal. "We need to study the origin of life in order to make sense of life itself, to see its possibilities and its limitations, and, hence, see how to promote the one and overcome the other. In a broader sense, the study of its origins is a further attempt to get meaning out of life."[5] Both Calvin and Bernal, in engagingly personal terms, outline their own experiences of the search for the meaning of human existence. Calvin's account is particularly candid. He writes of the social problems engendered by science and technology; of the age of Big Brother, described by Orwell, as being all too evident today; and of the impersonal tyranny of numbers as the world's population expands. Erwin Chargaff in his epilogue to a review on DNA takes up the refrain in an even more sombre tone. "The asinine prognostications of instant happiness through mail-order eugenics . . . may be counted among the symptoms of the onset of barbarism, as evidenced by the brutalisation of humanity; the overpopulation; the lack of foodstuffs; the pollution of everything that surrounds us, and even more of everything that is within us; the vulgarisation of artistic and scientific imagination."[6] The charge cannot be laid at the door of education or the lack

---

3. Bernal, J. D. (1967) *The Origin of Life.* Weidenfeld and Nicolson. P. 172, 182.
4. Calvin, M. (1969) *Chemical Evolution.* Oxford. Clarendon Press. p. 251.
5. Ref. 3, p. 163.
6. Chargaff, E. (1968) in *Prog. in Nuc. Acid Res. and Mol. Biol.* Davidson, J. N. and Conn, W. E. (eds.) 8, 297.

of it; it turns out that the problem of man is man himself.

THE TELEOLOGY CONNECTION

Teleology—as meaning goals and motives driving collections of molecules to form living systems—has for long been scientifically suspect when invoked to explain the origin of such systems. For it is not "explanation" in the scientific traditions at their thoroughgoing, experimental best. Nonetheless, teleology should not be rejected as without relevance or meaning to our discussions. For one thing, scientists are themselves not too sure that the familiar principles of scientific thinking applied to the question of origins and of evolution are impeccable. Marjorie Grene has posed the problem in a trenchant way. "The concept of evolution as identified with progressive adaptation is basically ambiguous.

"On the one hand, such adaptations are supposed to be mechanically self-generating—through mutation, natural selection, recombination, and isolation—and so to entail no teleological reference. Yet on the other hand, adaptation, like its Victorian twin 'utility,' is itself a teleological concept; it is adjustment to something for some end . . . . But the 'end' for Darwinism, dare not be some 'higher' form of life, the next 'level' to which evolution aspires: that would be to reintroduce a forbidden version of scientific 'teleology.' It must then, and is usually said to, be survival that adaptation is 'for.' But in that case the whole 'theory' becomes a tautology, a complicated way of saying simply that what survives survives."[7,8] Apart

---

7. Grene, M. (1969) in *Toward a Theoretical Biology*. Addington, C. H. (ed.) Edinburgh University Press. p. 61.
8. Neo-Darwinian principles have been challenged on mathematical and biological grounds as well. See *Mathematical Challenges to the Neo-Darwinian Interpretation of Evolution*. Moorehead, P. S. and Kaplan, M. M. (eds.). The Wistar Institute Press. (1967) See also *Implications of Evolution*. Kerkut, G. A. Pergamon Press. Oxford. (1960). The introduction of *The Origin of Species* by Charles Darwin. Thompson, W. R. J. M. Dent and Sons. (1956).

from espousing teleology in some form or other it is hard to see how circular reasoning of this sort may be avoided. As we have seen, the mechanisms of change and variability in biological evolution are being applied to chemical evolution. Though they may be conceptually related these mechanisms must be said to obtain in the latter with even less logical persuasiveness. Here teleology is found in the guise of **"looking aheadness"** and **"rootedness"** (Kenyon)[9] or **"expediency"** (Oparin).[10] "When science fails us," Unger writes, " 'biotheologic' inference and common sense may provide the best available basis for a guess." Unger was writing on a reaction of the human body to a high concentration of blood glucose, surmising that "nature's efforts are seldom purposeless."[11] E. B. Chain has put forward some refreshingly forthright views. "To postulate, as the positivists of the end of the last century and their followers have done, that the development and survival of the fittest is **entirely** a consequence of chance mutations, or even that nature carries out experiments by trial and error through mutations in order to create living systems better fitted to survive, seems to me a hypothesis based on no evidence and irreconcilable with the facts. This hypothesis willfully neglects the principle of teleological purpose which stares the biologist in the face wherever he looks, whether he is engaged in the study of different organs in one organism or even of different subcellular compartments in relation to each other in a single cell, or whether he studies the interrelation and in-

---

9. Kenyon, D. H. (1974) in *The Origin of Life and Evolutionary Biochemistry*. Dose, K., Fox, S. W., Deborin, G. A., and Pavlovskaya, T. E. Plenum Press. New York and London. p. 207.
10. Oparin, A. I. (1975) *Biology Bulletin of the Academy of Sciences of the USSR* (Translated from Russian). Consultants Bureau. New York. 2, 1.
11. Unger, R. H. (1976). "Diabetes and the Alpha Cell" (The Banting Memorial Lecture, 1975). *Diabetes*, 25, 136.

teractions of various species."[12]

One can, of course, bravely cut the Gordian knot of scientific teleology and elevate neo-Darwinian postulates of chance mutation and natural selection to the realm of axiomatic truths. If true this deprives us of the need to say anything further. Harris has tried to show that this is possible by the postulates satisfying a set of criteria. But the fact is these criteria have not been satisfied.[13] In a way Harris is merely expressing a disenchantment that is gradually setting in. Gone are the hopes of a quick laboratory *tour de force* which convincingly demonstrates how small biological molecules will somehow arrange themselves in mute obedience to known chemico-physical laws to produce larger molecules which, in turn, should acquire lifelike associations. It has not been a straightforward chemical problem.

SEPARATING THE RICE FROM THE CHAFF

It seems customary to speak of the beneficial effects of evolutionary principles on different branches of human endeavour and to suggest that through the order and cooperation that have somehow produced life and moulded it over aeons of time, great new accomplishments are in store for human society. In fact it is mooted that cultural evolution will take over and surpass anything that biological evolution has done for our species. So far as espousing evolutionary principles is considered necessary equipment for a "proper" scientific outlook, we are in hearty agreement with Sir Macfarlane Burnet. For some years he has been advocating the concept of an evolutionary approach to the problem of immunological surveillance, but he also qualifies his stand. "The concept is a broad unifying one that is not directly susceptible to experimental test. It can only be justified by its usefulness

---

12. Chain, E. B. (1971) *Perspect. Biol. Med.* 14, 347.
13. Harris, C. L. (1975) *Perspect. Biol. Med.* 18, 179.

as an aid to understanding and interrelating a wide range of experimental and clinical phenomena and from its power to satisfy the urge of any biologically-minded investigator to bring the field that interests him into an evolutionary framework."[14] Without the evolutionary framework scientific research can continue to flourish. Man can still look for cures to diseases, send rockets into space, and excel in other technological advances. At the social level, the evolution-based optimism, though admirable, is likely to prove naive, as we have seen. In a penetrating analysis of the impact of Darwin on social evolution Leibowitz observed that though his theories stimulated much new research in the life sciences, the effects of social Darwinism "not only led to doctrines of social and sexual superiority, but introduced into social theorising an anomalous philosophic base, which denied or diminished the utility of cultural analyses of social events."[15]

Echoes of Social Darwinism are being heard today, its critics would say, in the new "sociobiology." It looks as if every new generation must learn its own lesson and that history teaches us that history teaches us nothing.[16,17,18] Scientists may say that it is not their fault if their evolutionary theories have been abused. They ought to ask those whose social guide-lines are based on the theory. They are honestly working out the logical consequences of evolutionary thought. They form the sociological arm of evolutionary predestination.

---

14. Burnet, F. M. (1970) in *Immunity and Tolerance in Oncogenesis*. Severi, L. (ed.). Division of Cancer Research, Perugia, Italy. Vol. 1, p. XLV.
15. Leibowitz, L. (1969) *J. Theoret. Biol.* 25, 255.
16. Wilson, E. (1976) *New Sci.* 70, 342.
17. Lewin, R. (1976) *ibid.* p. 344.
18. Paper by Science as Ideology Group of the British Society for Social Responsibility in Science. *ibid.* p. 346.

CONCLUSION

Today life moves at such a speed that we are all concerned about where it is heading and whether it is assuming the qualities that are desirable. Progress in the various fields of human endeavour has brought problems in its train. This is not unexpected and these problems are being tackled with vigour. But more than ever before, man is compelled to search for meaning and significance in areas of personal, professional, and social involvement. He needs to know his ultimate origin in order to find a purpose for living and to see the purpose reflected, however dimly, in the broader life of the world around him. If that origin is sought in the primeval chaos, from whose random motions life is said to have spewed forth, then no satisfying meaning will likely be found. A tremendous amount of money and effort has been channeled along the lines of trying to demonstrate the plausibility of the chemical evolution of life. An impressive amount of data has accumulated. The fact remains that the probability that vital processes could have arisen and developed without directive forces is exceedingly small. Incredibly small, many would say; but that depends on where one has fixed one's cut-off value for credibility. The scientist, who so desires, may keep faith with the tenets of his training and yet find, as many have done, that meaning and significance will emerge as he acknowledges the wisdom of his Creator.

For thou didst form my inward parts,
 thou didst knit me together in my mother's womb.
I praise thee, for thou art fearful and wonderful
 Wonderful are thy works!
Thou knowest me right well;
 my frame was not hidden from thee,
when I was being made in secret,
 intricately wrought in the depths of the earth.
Thine eyes beheld my unformed substance;
 in thy books were written, every one of them,

the days that were formed for me,
    when as yet there was none of them.
How precious to me are thy thoughts, O God!
    How vast is the sum of them!

Psalm 139[13-17]

Chapter 9

An Update

Perhaps the appearance of life on the earth is a miracle. Scientists are reluctant to accept that view, but their choices are limited; either life was created on the earth by the will of a being outside the grasp of scientific understanding, or it evolved on our planet spontaneously, through chemical reactions occurring in non-living matter lying on the surface of the planet.

The first theory places the question of the origin of life beyond the reach of scientific inquiry. It is a statement of faith in the power of a Supreme Being not subject to the laws of science.

The second theory is also an act of faith. The act of faith consists in assuming that the scientific view of the origin of life is correct, without having concrete evidence to support that belief.

Robert Jastrow (1977)[1]

THE EARLY EARTH

It is well known that the laboratory synthesis of amino acids is inhibited by even small amounts of molecular oxygen. This has led investigators of the origin of life to postulate that the primitive atmosphere was reducing, a stringent requirement said to be supported by geological evidences. Appeals to this continue to be made in several publications.[2,3] Pettijohn keeps an open mind on the proposition of an oxygen-free early atmosphere and offers alternative explanations to the geologic evidences often cited.[4]

1. The absence of red colour in the earliest Precambrian sediments may only reflect, he says, the fact that much

---

1. *Until the Sun Dies.* Robert Jastrow. W. W. Norton & Co. Inc. New York (1977). pp. 62-63.
2. Schopf, J. W. (1978) *Sci. Am.* 239, 85.
3. Watson, A. J. and Lovelock, J. E. (1980) *BioSystems,* 12, 124.
4. *Sedimentary Rocks.* Pettijohn, F. J. Harper & Row. New York, Evanston, San Francisco, and London. 3rd edition (1976). p. 596.

of the Archaean sedimentary record is flyschlike. The flysch facies is not red; red coloration being more typical of terrestrial sediments.

2. The high ferrous-ferric iron ratio in early Precambrian slates and graywackes may be related more to metamorphic reductions rather than a reducing atmosphere.

3. The deposition of sulphide and sideritic sediments have been noted to occur in times of existence of large and varied life forms. An oxygen-rich atmosphere is not ruled out by their presence.

SYNTHESIS OF MONOMERS AND PROTOCELLS

Reports of the synthesis of amino acids and related monomers include those of Egami and Hatanaka.[5] Hydroxylamine and formaldehyde were heated in modified sea water medium under nitrogen and in the presence of transition metals and clays. Amino acid analysis by column chromatography gave products with retention times corresponding to 40 species of amino acids. Of these glycine, alanine, serine, and β-alanine were confirmed by single-dimension thin-layer chromatography. Oligomers with molecular weights in the range 200-1000 were resistant to pronase hydrolysis. A similar finding had been made previously by Ferris, et al, of oligomers derived from HCN (p. 26). Dillon has reviewed the field of synthetic advances and has made the following noteworthy remarks.[6]

1. One category of molecules which has rarely been synthesised is the lipids, without which cell membranes could not exist.

---

5. Hatanaka, H. and Egami, F. (1977). *Bull. Chem. Soc.* (Japan) 50, 1147.

6. *The Genetic Mechanism and the Origin of Life.* Dillon, L. S. Plenum Press. New York and London. (1978). pp. 1-64.

2. In the experimental production of the basic molecules the conditions vary over broad limits. One difficulty is the requirement for strongly basic or acidic conditions. The waters on earth today are most frequently mildly alkaline.

3. The large quantities of specialised condensing agents are unrealistic from a biological standpoint. These agents have left no trace of their existence in extant organisms.

4. The orderly sequence of reactions carried out in the laboratory on measured quantities of selected amino acids would, in real life, be rare accidents indeed.

5. Assuming that natural building blocks (e.g. L amino acids, D sugars) were somehow produced in quantity they must be quickly used before they convert into their biologically inactive mirror-images.

6. No proteins or nucleic acids have been synthesised in the laboratory under prebiotic conditions even in small amounts.

Methods to separate racemates are of obvious importance. A number of racemates can be resolved into optically pure enantiomers by chromatography on optically active absorbents such as amide, amino acid, and crown ether groups.[7] In recent work on crown ethers the aim has been to design host-guest systems capable of maximum chiral recognition. Tundo and Fendler have observed modest chiral recognitions using glycine-L-phenylalanine (Gly-L-Phe) and glycine-D-phenylalanine (Gly-D-Phe).[8] The translation of these findings into an abiotic environment is needed. Open chain analogues of the crown ethers are worth exploring, that is, the oligo (ethylene glycol dimethyl ethers). Also methods of differential crystallisation with seeding holds special promise because of their very simplicity.[9]

---

7. Blaske, G. (1980). *Angew. Chem. Int. Ed. Engl.* 19, 13.
8. Tundo, P. and Fendler, J. H. (1980) *J. Am. Chem. Soc.* 102, 1760.
9. Collet, A., Brienne, M.-J., Jacques, J. (1980) *Chem. Rev.* 80, 215.

It is significant that Dickerson's recent paper on chemical evolution and the origin of life could do little more than list the products of spark discharge experiments.[10] The paper has an extended discussion on the attempts of Fox and Oparin to form "proto-cells." Any comparison between the putative first "living" organisms on earth and Clostridia must be regarded as fanciful. For one thing Clostridial cell walls are made of phosphatidylethanolamine of the plasmalogen type and we have seen that the abiotic synthesis of even simple lipids is annoyingly elusive. The biochemical wherewithal of the Clostridia is truly impressive. They possess the Emden-Meyerhoff pathway enzymes, can ferment glucose to a variety of products. They deaminate glycine to yield acetate and extract energy by a unique process, the Strickland mechanism, which enables them to couple oxidation-reduction reactions between suitable pairs of amino acids. The strict anaerobe, Clostridium kluyveri, forms pyruvate by carboxylating acetyl-CoA. This involves the participation of ferredoxin and nicotinamide adenine dinucleotide (NAD).[11]

Surfactant vesicles mimicking cells are made by sonic dispersal of a host of chemicals which include dialkyl phosphates,[12] sulphonates, carboxylates,[13] and single-chain fatty acids. Fairly stable vesicles have been obtained with dioctadecyldimethylammonium chloride (DODAC). These cationic vesicles evince intermolecular energy transfer when a donor, lyopyrene, is incorporated into the membrane with the acceptor, pyranine. Excitation by light at 345 nm results in enhanced emission of pyranine at 510

10. Dickerson, R. E. (1978). *Sci. Am.* 239, 62.
11. *Chemical Microbiology.* Rose, A. H.. Butterworths. London, Boston. (1976). pp. 212ff.
12. Kunitake, T., Okahata, Y. (1978). *Bull. Chem. Soc.* Japan 51, 1877.
13. Mortara, R. A., Quinia, F. H., Chaimovich, H. (1978) *Biochem. Biophys. Res. Commun.* 81, 1080.

nm, parallel with a decrease in lyopyrene emission.[14] These same vesicles have also been used in light-induced photochemical energy conversion akin to that seen in photosynthesis. Electron transfer is followed by separation of charged products across the membrane. The investigators intend to improve on their models by entrapping chlorophyll and colloidal redox catalysers in the vesicles.[15]

MICROFOSSILS AND THE CONCEPT OF GEOLOGICAL TIME

Stromatolites are fossilised reefs, thin-layered limestone rock built up of organisms resembling blue-green algae and bacteria. In 1978 Schopf reported the oldest stromatolites as 3×10^9 years with the oldest discrete fossil-like organisms at 3.4×10^9 years.[16] A distinctive chert has been discovered in the Pilbara region of Western Australia which contain unbranched conical, columnar stromatolites.[17,18] The possible age range for these biogenic structures is 3.4 to 3.1×10^9 years. "If these and other Archaean stromatolites represent, at least in part, the activities of blue-green algae, as seem probable based on comparison with modern stromatolites, including Conophyton, they would substantiate suggestions that photosynthesis was an effective source of oxygen 3.5×10^9 years ago. They also imply that the origin of terrestrial life lies further back in geological time than 3.5×10^9 years."[19]

---

14. Nomura, T., Escabi-Perez, J. R., Sunamoto, J., and Fendler, J. H. (1980). *J. Am. Chem. Soc.* 102, 1484.
15. Infelta, P. O., Gratzel, M., and Fendler, J. H. (1980). *J. Am. Chem. Soc.* 102, 1479.
16. Ref. 2, p. 102.
17. Lowe, D. R. (1980). *Nature,* 284, 441.
18. Walter, M. R., Buick, R., and Dunlop, J. S. R. (1980). *Nature,* 284, 443.
19. Ref. 17, p. 442.

It is an intriguing point that other fossils are beginning to be found earlier in the geological time scale. Vertebrate fossils older than the Middle Ordovician (about 450×10^6 years) were unknown. In 1978 the remains of a heterostracan fish (class Agnatha) was discovered which extends the age of the earliest known vertebrate fossil by approximately 40×10^6 years.[20] Consider also the finding of "hominid footprints" in the Laetolil Beds of Tanzania. These prints already exhibit fully upright, bipedal, and free-striding gait.[21] Perhaps the absolute dating methods dependent on radionuclide decay require a reexamination as to their reliability.[22] The existence of plutonium halos in rocks certainly throws new light upon cosmological and geological concepts of the earth's origin.[23,24]

SYNTHETIC ENZYMATIC ACTIVITY

Interest continues to be focussed on the design of chemical analogues capable of functioning like biological molecules. The way the natural iron-containing oxygen carriers haemoglobin, myoglobin, and their cobalt derivatives carry oxygen poses a challenge to man's ingenuity. The reversibility of binding by the natural protein owes to the fact that the metal-porphyrin group is located in a hydrophobic protein pocket. Imitating this, a "dry" pocket is constructed by covering the synthetic ligands with a bridging group, $[-N(CH_3)-(CH_2)_6-(CH_3)N-]$. With this bridge synthetic cobalt (II) complexes bind oxygen in a manner almost equivalent to that of coboglobin.[25] This

20. Repetski, J. E. (1978). *Science,* 200, 529. See also Harper, D. A. J. (1979). *Nature,* 278, 634.
21. Leakey, M. D. and Hay, R. L. (1979). *Nature,* 278, 317.
22. Hedges, R. E. M. (1979). *Nature,* 281, 19.
23. Gentry, R. V. (1973) *Annu. Rev. Nucl. Sci.* 23, 347.
24. Gentry, R. V. (1974) *Science,* 184, 62.
25. Stevens, J. C. and Busch, D. H. (1980) *J. Am. Chem. Soc.* 102, 3285.

constitutes a great advance over model systems based on modified porphyrin structures used by other workers.

Kenner and his group at Liverpool embarked on a painstaking task of synthesising the enzyme lysozyme, or rather an analogue of it, consisting of 129 residues. The general plan was to divide the sequence into 12 sections each having glycine at the C terminus to avoid risk of racemisation. This is a species of labour not usually performed, but it has led to important improvements in chemical techniques from which, doubtless, future attempts will benefit.[26] More to our point is the goal of Sir John Cornforth in finding an olefin-hydrating catalyst, that is, a synthetic organic compound that will add a hydrogen and a hydroxyl group across a double bond. An example of an enzyme doing this would be fumarate hydratase which converts fumarate to malate. Such a catalyst would be, of course, economically worth finding.[27] The catalyst should be rigid with a non-polar cavity to fit the olefin. Within the cavity would lie a well-placed acidic group to effect the hydration. The answer appears to be found with the chemical family of substituted dibenzophospholes. An understanding of the fine architecture of the active sites of enzymes will stimulate synthetic work in this field. X-ray crystallographic studies are expected to contribute to the venture.[28]

PHYLOGENY AT THE CROSSROAD

Placing phylogeny on a firm molecular footing is a topical subject of research. To check for anomalies, that is, to test for congruence, is an area of interest. For this purpose it has been proposed that the evolutionary trees be constructed from sequences of several different gene products from a set of organisms. Non-congruence of

26. Kenner, G. W. (1977) *Proc. R. Soc. Lond. B.* 197, 237.
27. Cornforth, J. R. (1978) *Proc. R. Soc. Lond. B.* 203, 101.
28. James, M. N. G. (1980) *Canad. J. Biochem.* 58, 251.

evolutionary trees for Desulfovibrio and Clostridium ferredoxin and rubredoxin has already been noted.[29] Furthermore Ambler and his colleagues have found variation in cytochrome c_2 sequence among purple nonsulphur photosynthetic bacteria (Rhodospirillaceae).[30] They also draw attention to anomalies in amino acid sequences of small cytochromes c and cytochromes c′ from two species of purple photosynthetic bacteria.[31] Woese, however, has criticised the choice of the three types of proteins Ambler used in coming to the conclusion that molecular information is of little value in deciphering bacterial phylogeny. (Ambler believes in the possibility of lateral transfer of genes having scrambled the genetic record.) Woese would rather use a group of large molecules such as 16S rRNAs because this maintains functional and structural constancy over the group of organisms considered. Woese is joined by Dickerson[32] in the opinion that the standard taxonomy in Bergey's Manual[33] is not a dependable basis for classifying the Rhodospirillaceae; recourse should be made to molecular data. The last word has not been said on the matter. Novotny′ and Vitek consider that different phylogenies among homologous proteins could arise from structural variation. For instance, with cytochrome c_2 differing phylogenies can be derived from different structural segments of the molecule—the phylogeny of the whole being a weighted average.[34]

29. Bruschi, M. and LeGall, J. in *Evolution of Protein Molecules.* Matsubara, H. and Yamanaka, T. (eds.) Japan Sci. Soc. Press. (1978). pp. 221-232.
30. Ambler, R. P., Daniel, M., Hermoso, J., Meyer, T. E., Bartsch, R. G. and Kamen, M. D. (1979). *Nature,* 278, 659.
31. Ambler, R. P., Meyer, T. E., and Kamen, M. D. (1979). *Nature,* 278, 661.
32. Dickerson, R. E. (1979), *Nature,* 283, 210.
33. *Bergey's Manual of Determinative Bacteriology.* Buchanan, R. E. and Gibbons, N. E. (eds.) Williams and Wilkins. Baltimore. 8th edition. (1974).
34. Novotny′, J. and Vitek, A. (1980), *Nature,* 286, 309.

MINIMUM PHYLOGENETIC TREES

A variation of the minimum mutation distance procedure (p. 117) has been employed to construct "minimal phylogenetic trees." It requires the initial conversion of amino acid sequences into nucleotide sequences. These nucleotide codings are used to construct a tree with methods based on a partitioning theorem. The rule is that the number of nucleotide substitutions in the final tree is to be minimum, the smallest number of changes that will connect all the sequences.[35] The codings are revised whenever this leads to a decrease in the total length of the tree. An example of its use is provided by an optimal tree for ten mammalian haemoglobin α-chain sequences. The work is to be extended by using five different polypeptides for eleven species. It can be seen that this method is capable of greater accuracy when the amino acid-to-nucleotide transformation is eliminated through a direct knowledge of the DNA sequences. With advances in rapid DNA sequencing that day should not be far off.

A major limitation of the method is that while no "shorter tree" can link a set of data than the one presented, other equally short trees of different configuration may exist. The authors conclude: "It is unwise to claim too much biological significance for the one protein used. For this reason any biological conclusion should be avoided, except to mention that the primates form a natural group in all cases and the rodents (as represented by the mouse) are more closely related to the primates than to any other groups studied."[36] Any method using an amino acid-nucleotide transformation needs to take account of nucleotide transition probabilities. At a specified

35. Foulds, L. R., Hendy, M. D., and Penny, D. (1979). *J. Mol. Evol.* 13, 127-150, 151-167.
36. Penny, D., Hendy, M. D., and Foulds, L. R. (1980). *Biochem. J.* 187, 65.

locus in a gene any of the following twelve replacements
are possible.

$$A \longrightarrow C, G \text{ or } T$$
$$C \longrightarrow A, G \text{ or } T$$
$$G \longrightarrow A, C \text{ or } T$$
$$T \longrightarrow A, C \text{ or } G$$

(A = adenine, C = cytosine, G = guanine, T = thymine)

The four bases A, C, G, T are not present in equimolar
ratios of 25% each; all transitions are not equiprobable. If
that were so an equilibrium composition of A:C:G:T =
1:1:1:1 for DNA would result. The direction of the transi-
tion, e.g. A $\longrightarrow$ C or C $\longrightarrow$ A affects the frequency
values. Holmquist and Cimino have presented a method
of "maximum entropy inference" for the correct estima-
tion of various evolutionary parameters provided the
available experimental data are accurate and complete.[37]
Tables of the probabilities of nucleotide transition have
been worked out for the α-haemoglobin, β-haemoglo-
bin, myoglobin, cytochrome c, and the parvalbumin
group genes. The data base for the calculations are the
average amino acid composition of these five protein
families and the average nucleotide composition of their
coding genes at various codon loci. Only in the case of
β-haemoglobin are experimental values calculated from
the known mRNA sequences of human and rabbit
β-haemoglobin at the 119 codon loci known to have
varied. It will be necessary to look at DNA or mRNA data
from many sequences before the usefulness of this
method can be assessed.

PROTEINS AS A GUIDE TO EVOLUTION

The serine proteases form a natural group (p. 83). The
core tripeptide Asp-His-Ser occurs in many endopep-

---

37. Holmquist, R. and Cimino, B. J. (1980). *BioSystems*, 12, 1

tidases from a variety of organisms ranging from bacteria to man. The "gut hormones" (e.g. gastrin, cholecystokinin, caerulein, glucagon, secretin, vasoactive intestinal peptide, substance P, insulin, the enkephalins) fall into groups when considered from the point of view of similarities in amino acid sequences.[38,39] The question is: are these proteins linked evolutionarily or have we, all the while, been only delineating functional relationships? On the other hand we have proteins which are unrelated apparently in function but bear resemblances to each other for segments of their molecule. Are these sharing a common pedigree? Some examples from the large number of proteins found in serum illustrate the point. Haptoglobin, a protein which binds haemoglobin, is said to be related to the light chain of the immunoglobin through its constituent α_2 chain.[40] Curiously haptoglobin is also shown by the criterion of segment comparison to look like α_1 acid glycoprotein.[41] A protein belonging to the complement system, C1q (MW 400,000) bears a striking resemblance to collagen. Its three types of chains possess regions of about 80 amino acids close to the N-terminal abundant with the collagen triplet Gly-X-Y.[42] Hydroxyproline or hydroxylysine is often found in position Y. Factor B belongs to the alternative pathway of complement activation. Its active fragment contains the active proteolytic site of the C3 and C5 convertases, both of which have trypsinlike specificities. The partial amino sequence of this fragment, however, reveals little structural similarity between its amino terminal and that of the light chain of human C̄1r, C̄1s, plasmin, Factor B̄, or any of the other known serine proteases.[43] Vitellogenin is a protein synthesised in

38. *Gut Hormones*. Bloom, S. R. and Polak, J. M. (eds.) Churchill Livingston (1981).
39. Dockray, G. J. (1979). *Annu. Rev. Physiol.* 41, 83.
40. Black, J. A. and Dixon, G. H. (1968). *Nature,* 218, 736.
41. Schmid, K. (1972). *Chimia,* 26, 405.
42. Porter, R. R. and Reid, K. B. M. (1978). *Nature,* 275, 699.
43. Niemann, M. A., Volanakis, J. E. Nagasawa, S., and Lint, T. F. (1979). *Immunochem. Proteins,* 3, 167.

the livers of egg-laying vertebrates and transported to the egg. Chicken vitellogenin has been resolved into two species (VTG I and VTG II) by polyacrylamide gel electrophoresis in sodium dodecyl sulphate. Limited proteolysis of the two vitellogenins followed by electrophoresis indicate extensive differences betweeen VTG I and VTG II. Immunological data suggest little or no homology between them although they are, by physical properties, vitellogenins.[44]

GENE STRUCTURE AND FUNCTION

Evidence suggests the possibility that the well-known B-DNA conformation, a right-handed double helix, may not be a regular feature. A Z-form may interrupt the B-form. The repeating unit is a dinucleotide in the Z-form rather than a single nucleotide and the whole is a left-handed structure. The part played by Z-DNA in supercoiling, its interactions with DNA-specific enzymes and binding proteins are being examined.[45] Mention has been made of the natural internucleotide $3' \longrightarrow 5'$ phosphate linkage (p. 59). The finding of a natural $2' \longrightarrow 5'$ linkage of course arouses interest. Could it be the remnant of an ancient unusual oligonucleotide? An inhibitor of protein synthesis in interferon-treated cells has been identified as the 5'-triphosphate of adenosyl-$(2' \longrightarrow 5')$-adenyl-$(2' \longrightarrow 5')$-adenosine.[46] The synthetase enzyme for this unusual trinucleoside pentaphosphate has been isolated by chromatography on agarose poly(I)poly(C).[47] The oligonucleotide itself has also been chemically synthesised.[48]

44. Wang, S.-Y. and Williams, D. L. (1980) *Biochemistry,* 19, 1557.
45. Wang, A. H.-J., Quingley, G. J., Kolpak, F. J., Crawford, J. L., van Boon, J. H., van der Marel, G., and Rich, A. (1979) *Nature,* 282, 680.
46. Kerr, I. M. and Brown, R. E. (1978) *Proc. Natl. Acad. Sci. U.S.A.* 75, 256.
47. Hovanessian, A. G. and Kerr, I. M. (1978) *Eur. J. Biochem.* 84, 149.
48. Martin, E. M., Birdsall, N. J. M., Brown, R. E., and Kerr, I. M. (1979) *Eur. J. Biochem.* 95, 295.

The synthesis of protein beginning with DNA has been the subject of review.[49] The regulation of the processes were learned from the bacterium, E. coli, and it has been presumed that what is true of E. coli is true of elephants. Several investigators have found that there is, in higher organisms, no strict co-linear, uninterrupted relationship between a segment of DNA and the mRNA that comes from it. This is true of viruses as well. By implication it means that not all the DNA of the nucleus functions in the conventional coding sense. It also means that the DNA of a gene is discontinuous. It is broken up into parts by intervening "spacer" DNA, called "introns" by Gilbert.[50] The list of proteins, among eukaryotes, with discontinuous genes grows steadily and includes the genes for insulin, ovalbumin, immunoglobulin, lysozyme, tRNA genes of yeast and the β-globin gene of man.[51] The histone genes of the sea urchin (Psammechinus miliaris)[52] and the 5S genes of Xenopus paevis are not interrupted.[53]

It is clear now why the precursors of mRNA first appear as heterogeneous nuclear RNA (hnRNA). The hnRNA is the primary transcript of everything written along the DNA strand. By a process of cutting and splicing it is "edited" to yield the final product, mRNA. Questions multiply as quickly as these discoveries are made. What are the enzymes that perform the editing of hnRNA and what are the signals they recognise? It is obvious that the loss or inclusion of a single base as a result of a cut in the wrong place could completely scramble the rest of the message. Are there advantages in having so much "silent" DNA? How could informationally irrelevant genes, in the

49. From DNA to Protein. The Transfer of Genetic Information. Szekely, M. The Macmillan Press, Ltd. (1980).
50. Gilbert, W. (1978). Nature, 271, 501.
51. Flavell, R. A., Kooter, J. M., DeBeer, E., Little, P. F. R., and Williamson, R. (1978) Cell, 15, 25.
52. Schaffer, W., Kunz, G., Daetwyler, H., Telford, J., Smith, H. O., and Birnstiel, M. L. (1978) Cell, 14, 650.
53. Miller, J. R. and Brownlee, G. G. (1978). Nature, 275, 556.

first place, be introduced into pre-existing structural genes? There is no selective advantage in such a move. To say that the intervening sequences act to separate the genome so that there is a greater chance of shuffling the bits of genes during recombination is one conjecture. But there is more than a whiff of "teleology" in the statement (p. 167 ff). Whatever the answers to these questions eukaryotic gene expression has turned out to be more complicated than investigators could have predicted on the basis of the bacterial model. A variation of the discontinuous gene theme is also seen in embryonic and adult DNA. The DNA sequences coding for the variable and constant regions of the lambda light chain of mouse are separated by a long stretch of DNA in the embryo. They are in close proximity in bone marrow-derived lymphocytes.[54].

THE EVOLUTION OF THE GENOME

The chromosomes exist in such a fascinating variety of karyotypes that they are deservedly studied as to whether they are the cause of speciation or its consequence. The main kinds of changes said to have occurred are the doubling of entire genomes (polyploidy), gene duplication and deletion, structural rearrangement of the chromosomes, and plasmid-promoted genetic exchange.[55,56] The bacterial genome is assumed to evolve from small and simple to large and complex. It is not so much the origin of mutations, translocations, and inversions that is bothersome, but how they, being deleterious in effect, became fixed in a population. Bengtsson and Bodmer reach the conclusion that "in the absence of empirical data it is, unfortunately, impossible to separate the importance that

54. Rabbitts, T. H. and Foster, A. (1978) *Cell*, 13, 319.
55. *Modes of Speciation*. White, M. J. D. W. H. Freeman. San Francisco. (1978).
56. Riley, M. and Anilionis, A. (1978) *Ann. Rev. Microbiol.* 32, 519.

direct and indirect selection for chromosome mutations have in the evolution of karyotypes" but "that fixation of chromosome mutations by drift only occurs under special, and presumably very rare, circumstances."[57]

Bacteria subjected to a restricted growth milieu can acquire a capacity to metabolise novel substrates. This is not a de novo acquisiton of a new gene under selection pressure but a recruitment of existing enzymes that catalyse a similar reaction. An example is the recruitment of D-mannose isomerase in E. coli to utilise D-lyxose.[58] The genes for the enzymes are dormant, requiring a mutation to be expressed. It is begging the question to call these newly expressed enzymatic activities "evolutionary remnants."

The acquisition of extra genetic material is an interesting phenomenon. It can occur through either duplication of the cell's own DNA or transfer by plasmids from an outside source. Replicate genes are widely believed to be a convenient substrate for evolutionary forces to create divergence. Riley and Anilionis, however, state, "At present there is no formal proof for an evolutionarily significant instance of duplication and divergence."[56] Plasmids may be responsible for the interchange of genes between families and genera of bacteria, but Sanderson concludes that this did not greatly influence the course of evolution.[59] Exciting discoveries of the genome's influence on phenotype lie in the near future. Thus the basic characteristics between Escherichia, Pseudomonas, and Bacillus may derive from differences in gene arrangement and regulation rather than in nucleotide or protein sequences.

---

57. Bengtsson, B. O. and Bodmer, W. F. (1976) *Theor. Appl. Genet.* 9, 260.
58. Stevens, F. J. and Wu, T. T. (1976) *J. Gen. Microbiol.* 97, 257.
59. Sanderson, K. E. (1976) *Ann. Rev. Microbiol.* 30, 327.

THE ORIGIN OF MITOCHONDRIA
AND CHLOROPLASTS

Mention has been made of the conjecture that mitochondria were derived by endosymbiosis of prokaryotes (p. 130). Bacteria and blue-green algae took up symbiotic residence in a primitive eukaryote to yield mitochondria and chloroplasts respectively. Schwartz and Dayhoff have even found a place for the mythical "eukaryote mitochondrion" on the phylogenetic tree based on c-type cytochromes. It lies on the tree together with aerobic bacteria after their alleged divergence from the blue-green algae and chloroplasts.[60] The particular ancient bacterium which ultimately transformed into the mitochondrion was thought to be most closely related to the family of photosynthetic bacteria, the Rhodospirillaceae. This carries the inference that that bacterium was photosynthetic until shortly before or just after it invaded the protoeukaryote host. Other workers believe that an aerobic bacterium resembling Paracoccus became the mitochondrion.[61] In which case, the synthesis of the Paracoccus enzyme, nitrate reductase, would be repressed in the presence of oxygen. Using modern methods of genetic analysis it should theoretically be possible to locate evolutionary remnants of the enzyme in modern mitochondrial DNA.

An appeal is also made for the evidential value of the presence of certain large bacteria within the giant amoeba, Peleomyxa palustris.[61] These bacteria are made out to be a model of a transition stage in the evolution of mitochondria. It is true that this is an unusual site to find bacteria, but these organisms lie within well-demarcated vacuoles of the host cell. It is well known that even host structures lacking membranes are normally destroyed by its lysosomes as part of cellular housekeeping.

---

60. Schwartz, R. M. and Dayhoff, M. O. (1978) *Science*, 199, 395.
61. Whatley, J. M., John, P., and Whatley, F. R. (1979) *Proc. R. Soc. Lond. B* 204, 165.

Remarkably the bacteria divide in phase with the host cell and daughter cells of the host receive their share of the endosymbionts. The signals for this concerted division appear to be mediated by tubular connections between the vacuoles, wherein lie the bacteria, and the host's nuclear envelope.

Human mitochondrial tRNA sequences should provide interesting information on the possibilities of mitochondrial ancestry. It has been demonstrated, however, that the human tRNA sequences show no greater homology to prokaryotes than to eukaryotes. They seem to form a distinct class.[62] Furthermore the 12S rRNA of human mitochondria lacks the polypurine-complementary sequence (CCUGC) found in prokaryotes. It is known that E. coli aminoacyl tRNA synthetases are unable to charge human mitochondrial tRNAs.[63] Eperon and his colleagues are led to conclude that, for human mitochondrial RNA, "the extent of the differences from other rRNA genes has consequences for the mechanism of initiation of protein synthesis and argues, at least, for a more ancient origin of any symbiosis than 'recent common ancestry'[60] with prokaryotes or eukaryotes."

As chloroplasts are varied in their photosynthetic pigments and thylakoid structure they are envisaged as having three or more different ancestral symbionts.

Cytochrome c oxidase, the terminal oxidase of the respiratory chain in eukaryotes, has been shown to consist of seven subunits. In all organisms studied cytochrome c oxidase is a chimera of protein units synthesised at two sites—the mitochondrion and cytoplasm. Work on human placental mitochondria confirms and extends the previous findings.[64] Keeping in mind the phylogenetic antiquity at-

62. Eperon, I. C., Anderson, S., and Nierlich, D. P. (1980) *Nature,* 286, 460.
63. Martin, R. P. (1978) *Nucleic Acids Res.* 5, 4579.
64. Hare, J. F., Ching, E., and Attardi, G. (1980) *Biochemistry,* 19, 2023.

tributed to this enzyme one is left wondering how its code came to partition itself between the mitochondrial and nuclear DNA. It is harder still to imagine a promiscuous plasmid as the perpertrator of the transfer to or from the mitochondrion.

THE ORIGIN OF THE GENETIC CODE

"The evolution of the genetic machinery is the step for which there are no laboratory models hence we can speculate endlessly, unfettered by inconvenient facts."
R. E. Dickerson (1978)[65]

Sorting out the alleged trail left by the genetic code as it evolved confronts us with that annoying bafflement so ably expressed by Popper (p. 55). Without exception every hypothesis suffers from the conceptual inadequacy of having to satisfy, at one and the same time, reasons as to why, and mechanisms as to how, information storage, retrieval, replication, and translation could have been achieved. Jukes take the view that "living organisms have evolved in a manner that took advantage of the composition of the genetic code, just as an individual species will adjust to an ecological niche."[66] This seems to be another way of saying that we are essentially back to where we started.

Proposals now favour the co-evolution of the code and the amino acid it serves.[65-70] Co-evolution suggests that the code arose together with a few easily-formed amino acids. These amino acids were the precursors for groups of synthetically related amino acids which then shared the

65. Dickerson, R. E. (1978) *Sci. Am.* 239, 62.
66. Jukes, T. H. (1978) *Adv. Enzymol.* 47, 375.
67. Wong, T. J. (1975) *Proc. Natl. Acad. Sci.* 72, 1909
68. Wong, T. J. (1976) *Proc. Natl. Acad. Sci.* 73, 2336.
69. Tremolieres, A. (1980) *Biochimie,* 62, 493.
70. *The Genetic Mechanism and the Origin of Life.* Dillon, L. S. Plenum Press. New York and London. (1978). pp. 211-344.

codons of their precursors, with some modifications. Wong suggests that about 3.5 billion years ago cells began with a highly ambiguous primitive code for about seven abundant amino acids from the primitive soup and achieved by about one billion years later a highly unambiguous code for twenty amino acids.[68] Tremolieres chooses an early family of four amino acids[69] and Dillon has five.[70]

Several observations may be made about the co-evolution model. It is really about the only way out of an impasse after more than a decade of debate. The finding of a natural fit between protein sequences and nucleic acid sequences might have helped to solve the problem. In the primitive cell, at least, tRNAs, ribosomes, and enzymes would then be redundant. No convincing evidence exists for such a direct protein-nucleic acid relationship. Saxinger and Ponnamperuma showed that direct reactions of different amino acids with oligonucleotides depend on the type of the acid and the relative length and not just the composition of the oligonucleotide.[71]

1. That the primitive cell should survive and extend its repertoire of four to seven amino acids is an impossible demand on biochemical virtuosity. On the co-evolution model we are to suppose the co-existence of charging enzymes (ligases) which attach the amino acids to simple tRNAs. The modern enzymes are sophisticated entities. They contain a region forming specific bonds with an amino acid and another region forming equally specific bonds with the tRNA that carry the amino acid. Most certainly these enzymes were constituted by a greater variety of amino acids than the few they were supposed to handle. How was this possible seeing that they as proteins needed to be reproduced themselves? Surely, in this instance, natural selection would admit of no piecemeal tinkering with the genetic apparatus.

71. Saxinger, C. and Ponnamperuma, C. (1974) *Origins LIfe,* 5, 189.

2. Important to the concept of co-evolution is the division of amino acids into groups. Groups 2 to 4 are derived from Group 1. It is conjectured that, for example, glutamate from Group 1 could be converted to glutamine, proline, arginine, leucine, and histidine, all members of Group 2. Similarly aspartate and alanine from Group 1 were ancestral to members of Groups 3 and 4. The argument for grouping the amino acids stems from the belief that there appears to be a predominant base for each of the four sets of codons corresponding to the four groups. Group 1 has guanine, Group 2, cytosine, Group 3, adenine, and Group 4, uracil. We see now that the proposed chemical syntheses are a Procrustean device to force a chemical relationship among members of the groups.[72] Ambiguities remain, however. Arginine is in both the cytosine and adenine groups, leucine in the cytosine and uracil groups, and serine in the uracil and adenine groups. Dual origins are thought to be responsible for these acids.

3. It has long been noted that the DNA codons and amino acids are not randomly matched. Sonneborn had proposed his lethal-mutation theory which sought to explain the fact that codons that are structurally similar often code for the same amino acid.[73] The substitution of one base for another frequently creates a triplet for the same or a structurally similar amino acid. This device (said to be a triumph of evolutionary strategy) minimises the harmful effects of chemical alteration to the bases or an accidental mismatch during information retrieval. The triplets for the hydrophobic amino acids isoleucine, leucine, methionine, phenylalanine, and valine are found to differ by only one base. The co-evolution theory has

---

72. Ref. 70, pp. 218-233.
73. Sonneborn, T. M. (1965) in Evolving Genes and Proteins. V. Bryson and H. J. Vogel (eds.) Academic Press. p. 377.

the effect of scattering the hydrophobic amino acids over all its four groups. Apparently two forces have shaped the code; their part in its origin is obscure as to their relative importance.

4. Methionine and tryptophan were late arrivals according to the co-evolution model.[68] These amino acids are nevertheless pivotal to construction of the cytochromes which are detected in extracts of many chemolithotrophic bacteria. This group of bacteria occupies an honoured place as one of the earliest organisms to appear because of their ability to obtain energy by oxidising inorganic compounds. As cytochromes of eukaryotes and prokaryotes differ but slightly, it is interesting to examine cyctochrome c. Lining the wall of the haem pocket is a methionine residue which fills the sixth octahedral position of the iron atom, the fifth coordination position being filled by the ring ε-nitrogen of a histidyl residue. Tryptophan is one of the invariant residues lining one of two hydrophobic channels leading from the haem group to the surface of the molecule.[74]

5. The time-table for co-evolution of the genetic code sets the formation of the primitive code for a few amino acids in protobionts at $> 3.5 \times 10^9$ years.[68] We have firm evidence that at this time biochemically complex organisms resembling blue-green algae were already in existence.[17,18]

Lagerkvist has put forward some interesting speculations of the evolution of the code rather than its origin. He starts from the stage when "the code has reached a degree of sophistication where four distinct bases were employed to code for an assortment of amino acids more limited than

---

74. Muirhead, H. (1974) in *Chemistry of Macromolecules. Biochemistry Series One.* Vol. 1. Gutfreund, H. (ed.) M.T.P. International Review of Science. Butterworths. University Park Press. p. 69.

that found in proteins today."[75] It makes no predictions as to which codon should code for which amino acid but addresses itself to the distribution of codons between "family" and "nonfamily" positions.

CONCLUSION

There is a refreshing candour among origin-of-life scientists today as they view the results of their work, both theoretical and experimental. Intractable problems remain that seem to defy solution. After all, though Darwinism is not a scientific theory, as Popper reminds us, "Its value for science as a metaphysical research programme is very great, especially if it is admitted that it may be criticised and improved upon."[76] Let Pollard, a theoretical physicist, who has examined the prevalence of Earth-like planets in our galaxy, have his say:

"There is a deeply ingrained conviction in the great majority of mankind, to which the appeal of science fiction and fantasy bears witness, that the universe is so constituted that if an opportunity exists for life to originate, it will be actualised, and if an opportunity exists for hominids to evolve, that too will be actualised. Whatever may be the basis for such convictions, it must clearly be sought outside the domain of science."[77]

---

75. Lagerkvist, U. (1980) Am Sci. 68, 192.
76. Unended Quest. Popper, K. Fontana. 1976.
77. Pollard, W. G. (1979) Am. Sci. 67, 653.

Index

A

NOTES